W9-ASC-146

$I \cdot B \cdot S$

ISAAC BASHEVIS SINGER

A DAY OF PLEASURE

Stories of a Boy Growing Up in Warsaw

WITH PHOTOGRAPHS BY ROMAN VISHNIAC

A SUNBURST BOOK
FARRAR, STRAUS AND GIROUX

HE stories I tell in this book actually took place during the first fourteen years of my life. Only the last story, "Shosha," deals with a later time, but it too concerns my childhood. I have a good deal more to tell about myself, my family, and the Poland of days gone by. I hope to continue these memoirs and reveal a world that is little known to you but which is rich in comedy and tragedy; rich in its individuality, wisdom, foolishness, wildness, and goodness.

Fourteen of these stories previously appeared, in somewhat different form, in my book of memoirs entitled *In My Father's Court*. Five are collected here for the first time: "Who I Am," "The Trip from Radzymin to Warsaw," "Reb Itchele and Shprintza," "The Mysteries of the Cabala," and "Shosha."

The stories were translated from my original Yiddish by Channah Kleinerman-Goldstein, Elaine Gottlieb, Elizabeth Shub, Elizabeth Pollet, Rosanna Gerber, and my nephew Joseph Singer.

I. B. S.

• PHOTOGRAPHS •

Except for those of Isaac Bashevis Singer, his brother, and his grandfather, the photographs were taken by Roman Vishniac between the time the Nazis came to power and the invasion of Poland in 1939. Nearly all of them were taken in Warsaw, a few in nearby towns. The world portrayed in these photographs is essentially the same as the one in the stories, even though the stories take place a generation earlier.

Who I Am

A tutor and a young scholar on the way to cheder

WAS born in the town of Radzymin, near Warsaw, the capital of Poland, on July 14, 1904. My father, Pinchos Menachem Singer, was a rabbi, a highly religious man. He had a red beard, long black sidelocks, and blue eyes. My mother, Bathsheba, was the daughter of the Rabbi of Bilgoray, which is not far from Lublin. She had red hair that she cut short and covered with a wig, as was the custom among pious married women.

Early in 1908, when I was three years old, my parents moved from Radzymin to Warsaw. There my father became a rabbi on a very poor street, Krochmalna. The tenement building where I grew up would be called a slum in America, but in those days we did not think it was so bad. At night a kerosene lamp lit our apartment. We were unfamiliar with such conveniences as hot running water or a bathroom. The outhouse was located in the courtyard.

Most of the people who lived on Krochmalna Street were poor storekeepers or laborers, but there were many scholars among them, as well as idle urchins, criminals, people from the underworld.

When I was about four years old, I began going to

5

cheder to study. A tutor would come every morning to take me there. I carried a prayer book with me, and later a Bible or a volume of the Talmud. These were the only schoolbooks I knew. In cheder we were taught mostly religion: to pray, to read the Pentateuch. We also learned to write Yiddish. My first teacher was an old man with a white beard.

I had a younger brother, Moshe, who was an infant when we moved to Warsaw; a sister, Hinde Esther, who was thirteen years older than I; and a brother, Israel Joshua, who was eleven years older. All of us except Moshe became writers. My brother's novel *The Brothers Ashkenazi* has been translated into several languages, including English. He wrote in Yiddish, just as I do.

Our house was a house of learning. My father sat all day long and studied the Talmud. Whenever my mother had a free minute, she glanced into a holy book. Other children had toys, but I played with my father's books. I started to "write" even before I knew the alphabet. I would dip a pen in ink and scribble. I also liked to draw—horses, houses, dogs. The Sabbath was an ordeal for me, because it is forbidden to write on that day.

In our Warsaw apartment my father set up a rabbinical court. The people of Krochmalna Street came to our home to ask him for advice or to have him settle a dispute according to the law of the Torah. In a sense he was a combination of rabbi, judge, and spiritual leader. People also came to him to pour out their hearts. My father presided at weddings in our apartment and from time to time he granted a divorce. Among Jews of that time, a rabbi was a man of many trades and few blessings.

I was curious by nature. I observed the grownups, their behavior. I listened attentively to their talk, which I sometimes understood and sometimes did not.

At an early age I started to think all kinds of thoughts: What would happen if a bird flew in the same direction forever? What would happen if a ladder were built from the earth to the sky? What was there before the world was created? Did time have a beginning? But how can time begin? Has space an end? But how can empty space have an end?

Our apartment at 10 Krochmalna Street had a balcony and I would stand on it for many hours and muse. In the summertime all kinds of insects gathered there—flies, bees, butterflies. These creatures provoked extreme curiosity in me. What do they eat? Where do they sleep? Who gave them life? At night the moon and the stars appeared in the sky. I was told that some stars are larger than the earth. But if they are so big, how can they fit in the narrow strip of sky above the roofs of Krochmalna Street? I often asked my parents questions that even they were at a loss to answer. My father used to say that it is not good to indulge in such questions. My mother would say that when I grew up I would find the answers. But I soon learned that even adults do not know everything. People died on our street and the shock of death awakened fear and wonder in me. My mother comforted me by saying that the good souls go to paradise after

7

death. But what do the souls *do* in paradise, I wanted to know. How does it look there? I brooded about the terrors of hell, where the souls of sinners are punished.

I was still young when I became aware of human suffering. Poland, torn and divided between Russia, Germany, and Austria, had lost its independence about one hundred years before. But we Jews had lost our land of Israel almost two thousand years before. My father assured me, however, that if the Jews conducted themselves piously, the Messiah would come and we would all return to the land of Israel. But two thousand years was too long to wait. Besides, how could you be sure that all the Jews would heed God's law? There were thieves on our street, all sorts of swindlers. Their kind could delay the coming of the Messiah forever . . .

The year I was born, a great Jewish leader died, Dr. Theodor Herzl. Dr. Herzl preached that the Jews must not wait for the coming of the Messiah but should start to build Palestine by themselves. But how could we do that when the land belonged to the Turks?

There were revolutionaries on our street who wanted to get rid of the Tsar of Russia. They dreamed about creating a state where all worked and there were no rich or poor. But how could anyone dethrone the Tsar when he had so many soldiers with swords and rifles? And how could there be no rich or poor? Some people would always have to live on Krochmalna Street and others would live on Marshalkovsky, a beautiful boulevard with trees and fancy stores. Some would live in big cities and others in distant villages. In our home these questions were often discussed by my family and visitors. I listened to every word.

My parents, my older brother, and my sister all liked to tell stories. My father would often tell of the miracles performed by various rabbis, also of ghosts, devils, imps. In this way he wanted to strengthen our belief in God and in the good and evil powers who reign in the world. My mother told us stories about Bilgoray, where her father was the rabbi and ran the community with a strong hand. My brother Joshua became worldly and started to read books that were not religious. He told me stories about Germany, France, America, about unfamiliar nations and races, about peculiar beliefs and customs. He described everything vividly, as if he had seen it for himself. My sister told romantic stories about counts who fell in love with servant girls. I had my own fantasies. At a very young age I began inventing all kinds of tales that I told the boys in cheder. Once I told them that my father was a king, and with such detail that they believed me. How they could have believed me is still a puzzle to me. I certainly was not dressed like a prince.

In 1914 the First World War began. In 1915, when I was eleven, the Germans occupied Warsaw. In 1917 I heard the extraordinary news that Tsar Nicholas II of Russia had been dethroned. The soldiers with the swords and rifles had not protected him; they themselves had backed the revolutionaries. If this could be so, was it also possible that soon there would be no rich or poor?

But apparently that time was still far away. In

1917 Warsaw was plagued by hunger and typhus. The Germans dragged people off the streets for forced labor. My family was starving, so it was decided that Mother and the younger children, Moshe and I, would go to our grandparents in Bilgoray, where the food shortage was not so severe. At that time I was thirteen, already a Bar Mitzvah boy, but I still had found no answers to any of my questions.

The Trip from Radzymin to Warsaw

In the Jewish neighborhood of Warsaw

THE little train began moving. I was sitting at the window, looking out. People seemed to be walking backwards. Horse-drawn carts rode in reverse. Telegraph poles were running away. Beside me sat my mother and my sister, Hindele, who held the baby on her lap, my brother Moshe. We were on the way from Radzymin to Warsaw.

My big brother, Joshua, was making the trip in the horse-drawn wagon that carried our furniture and ragged belongings. My father was already in Warsaw. He had rented an apartment at 10 Krochmalna Street, where he was to establish his rabbinical court.

The move from the small town of Radzymin to the big city of Warsaw was a burden and a problem for the family. But for me it was a joy. Each moment new experiences were revealed to me. The tiny locomotive (it was jokingly called "the samovar") whistled gaily. From time to time it let off steam and smoke just like a big locomotive. We rode past villages, huts with straw roofs, pastures where cows and horses grazed. One horse leaned its neck on another horse's neck. Scarecrows stood in the fields, dressed in tatters,

15

and birds circled them, cawing and screeching. I kept asking my mother questions. What is this? What is that? My mother and my sister answered me. Even strange women tried to explain things to me. But I still wasn't satisfied. I was possessed with curiosity and a thirst for explanation. Why do cows eat grass? Why does smoke come out of the chimney? Why does a bird have wings though a calf doesn't? Why do some people walk and others ride in wagons?

My mother shook her head. "The boy drives me crazy!"

The entire trip lasted barely two hours, but it left so many impressions that it seemed to me it was a long journey. The wonders increased as we neared Warsaw. Tall buildings with balconies emerged. We passed by a vast cemetery with thousands of tombstones. A red trolley car appeared. Factory buildings with high chimneys and barred windows loomed up. I realized that there was no longer any sense in asking questions and became silent. Then the little train stopped.

We took a droshky drawn by a gray horse. It rode over the Praga bridge and I was told the river beneath was the same Vistula that flowed in Radzymin. But how can the Vistula be so long, I asked myself. For the first time I saw boats and ships. One ship whistled and groaned so loudly that I had to cover my ears. On the deck of another, a band was playing. The brass instruments gleamed in the sun and dazzled me.

After we crossed the bridge, another wonder emerged, the monument of King Zygmunt. Four stone creatures, half man and half fish, were drinking from huge stone goblets. I was about to ask what this was, but before I could open my mouth new marvels turned up. Streets lined with huge buildings. Store windows displaying dolls that looked strangely alive. Ladies on the sidewalks wearing hats trimmed with cherries, peaches, plums, grapes. Some had veils covering their faces. I saw men with top hats who carried silver-handled canes. There were many red trolley cars, some drawn by horses, others horseless. My sister said these moved by electricity. I saw mounted policemen, firemen with brass helmets, carriages rolling along on rubber wheels. The horses held their heads high and had short tails. The driver of our droshky, who wore a blue coat and a cap with a shiny visor, spoke Yiddish. He pointed out the sights of Warsaw to us provincials.

I was both delighted and humbled. What value has a small boy, compared to such a great, tumultuous world? And how could we find Father here? And how would we locate my brother Joshua and the wagon with our furniture? It seemed that the adults knew everything. Apparently they had built all of this, while I, a small boy, sat there helplessly, with my sister holding my hand so I wouldn't fall. Whenever the droshky made a turn, the sky turned with it and my brain rattled in my head like a kernel in a nut.

All of a sudden the coachman said, "Here is Krochmalna Street."

The buildings there seemed even taller. The gutter was filled with people. The throngs, the yelling, the pushing reminded me of the fire I had witnessed in

17

Radzymin some weeks before and I was certain a fire had broken out here in Warsaw too. Boys shouted, jumped, whistled, and shoved one another. Girls laughed shrilly. Dusk was falling and a man who had a long stick with a flame on the end lit the street lamps. Women peddled all kinds of merchandise. Smoke curled from chimneys. The droshky drove up to the gate of a courtyard and I saw my brother Joshua. The wagon with the furniture had arrived before us.

My mother asked for Father, and Joshua answered, "He went to recite the evening prayer."

"Woe is me, this city is bedlam," she exclaimed.

"A gay street," my brother said.

"How come they're all outside?" my mother asked.

We entered the gate and went into our building. I was led up a stairway. I had never walked on steps before and climbing from one step to another seemed interesting and dangerous to me.

A woman met us on the staircase and said, "Are you the rabbi's wife? Woe, my God, you've been robbed from head to foot . . . A plague take the thieves, may a black fire consume their intestines. As soon as your things were unloaded, they dragged them away. Dear Father in heaven, may they be dragged to the cemetery!"

"Why didn't you watch?" my mother asked Joshua.

"You can't watch all of them. You start to argue with one and meanwhile ten others steal from you."

"Is any bedding left, at least?"

"They left something," he said.

"Jewish thieves?"

"There are few Gentiles here . . ."

A door opened and we entered a kitchen. The walls were painted pink. Then we walked into a large room with a window and a balcony. I went out on the balcony and I was both inside and outside at the same time. Downstairs the crowd milled. Up above, over the roofs, stretched a thin strip of sky. A moon hung in it, yellow as brass. Lamps glowed in all the windows, and when I narrowed my eyes to slits, fiery rays stretched out from them. Suddenly the din increased. A fireman came riding from somewhere, on a fast horse. His brass helmet glowed like fire. The boys started screaming: "The outrider, the outrider!"

Later on, I found out that the firemen were too often fooled on this street. They were frequently called when there was no fire, so a rider was sent to investigate. Yes, this time there really was a fire. Smoke billowed out of a window on a high floor and sparks flew. People filled the balconies. Wild horses harnessed to wagons arrived. Firemen ran into the building with hatchets, ladders, and rubber hoses. Policemen with swords chased the curious crowd.

In our apartment, my sister lit a kerosene lamp. My mother started to look through what was left of our belongings. "Yes, they stole," she said. What remained of our furniture was broken. Some of our Passover dishes were smashed.

Our new rooms smelled of paint and turpentine.

Singing voices drifted in from neighboring apartments. My brother said they came from gramophones. A cantor sang, as in the synagogue; a girl laughed; women quarreled; but none of this was real. All these voices came through giant trumpets on gramophones. My brother already knew who discovered all this : Edison from America.

"How can trumpets sing and talk?" my mother asked.

"You talk into them and they repeat what you say," Joshua explained.

"But how?"

"With a magnet . . ."

"It's all electricity," said my sister.

"The children should be put to sleep," my mother decided after a while.

I was undressed and I didn't resist. I was too tired. I was put to bed and fell asleep immediately. I opened my eyes and the room was flooded with sunlight. The windows stood open. The floor looked new. I walked out on the balcony. The same street that yesterday had been wrapped in night was now radiant in the sun. Customers pushed about in the stores. Men went off to pray with prayer-shawl bags under their arms. Sidewalk peddlers sold loaves of bread, baskets of bagels and rolls, smoked herring, hot peas, brown beans, apples, pears, plums. A boy drove a bevy of turkeys down the middle of the street. They tried to scatter but he trickily ran alongside with a stick and forced them to stay together.

My father was already sitting at his table, bent

over a volume of the Talmud. He noticed me and made me recite the prayer "I Thank Thee."

He said, "You will go to cheder here."

"I won't know the way."

"A tutor will take you there."

For breakfast my mother gave me food I had never tasted before: a bagel with cottage cheese and smoked herring. A neighbor came in and he started to tell us what had happened here during the 1905 revolution against the Tsar. The young revolutionaries shot off guns. All the stores had to be closed. Policemen struck the demonstrators with bare swords. Someone threw a bomb.

My mother shook her head sadly. My father tugged at his beard. A few years had already passed, but obviously the people of Krochmalna Street could not forget those days of terror. Many of the rebels were still imprisoned in the Citadel. Others had been sent off to Siberia. Many escaped to America.

My father asked, "What did they want?"

"To get rid of the Tsar."

My mother turned white. "I don't want the boy to hear of such goings on."

"What can he understand?" the neighbor said.

But I listened anyway. My curiosity had no limits.

A Day of Pleasure

A busy street lined with droshkies

HEN times were good, I would get a two-groschen piece, a kopeck, from Father or Mother every day, as every boy who went to cheder did. For me this coin represented all worldly pleasures. Across the street was Esther's candy store, where one could buy chocolates, jelly beans, ice cream, caramels, and all sorts of cookies. Since I had a weakness for drawing with colored pencils, which cost money, a kopeck proved not nearly so large a coin as Father and Mother made it out to be. There were times when I was forced to borrow money from a cheder classmate, a young usurer who demanded interest. For every four groschen, I paid a groschen a week.

Now imagine the indescribable joy I felt when I once earned a whole ruble—one hundred kopecks!

I no longer remember exactly how I came to earn that ruble, but I think it happened something like this: A man had ordered a pair of kidskin boots from a shoemaker, but upon delivery they proved to be either too tight or too loose. The man refused to accept them, and the shoemaker brought him to my father's rabbinical court. Father sent me to another shoemaker to ask him

27

to appraise the value of the boots or perhaps even to buy them, since he also dealt in ready-made footwear. It so happened that the second shoemaker had a customer who wanted the boots and was prepared to pay a good price for them. I do not recall all the details, but I remember that I carried a pair of brand-new boots around, and that one of the litigants rewarded me with a ruble.

I knew that if I stayed home my parents would ruin that ruble. They would buy me something to wear, something I would have got anyway, or they would borrow the ruble from me and—though they'd never deny the debt—I would never see it again. I therefore took the ruble and decided to indulge myself for once in the pleasures of this world, to enjoy all those good things for which my heart yearned.

I quickly passed through Krochmalna Street. Here everyone knew me too well. Here I could not afford to act the profligate. But on Gnoyna Street I was unknown. I signaled to the driver of a droshky, and he stopped.

"What do you want?"

"To ride."

"Ride where?"

"To the other streets."

"What other streets?"

"To Nalewki Street."

"That costs forty groschen. Have you got the money to pay?"

I showed him the ruble.

"But you'll have to pay me in advance."

I gave the driver the ruble. He tried bending it to see if it was counterfeit. Then he gave me my change —four forty-groschen pieces. I got into the droshky. The driver cracked his whip and I almost fell off the bench. The seat under me bounced on its springs. Passers-by stared at the little boy riding alone in a droshky, without any bundles. The droshky made its way among trolley cars, other droshkies, wagons, delivery vans. I felt that I had suddenly assumed the importance of an adult. God in heaven, if I could only ride like this for a thousand years, by day and by night, without stop, to the ends of the earth . . .

But the driver turned out to be a dishonest man. When we had gone only halfway, he stopped and said, "Enough. Get down!"

"But this is not Nalewki Street!" I argued.

"Do you want a taste of my whip?" he answered.

Oh, if only I were Samson the Strong, I'd know how to take care of such a bandit, such a clod! I would pulverize him, chop him into little pieces! But I am only a small weak boy, and he is cracking his whip.

I got down, shamed and dejected. But how long can you mourn when you have four forty-groschen pieces in your pocket? I saw a candy store and went in to select my merchandise. I bought some of every kind. And as I bought, I tasted. The other customers looked at me with disdain; they probably suspected I had stolen the money. One girl exclaimed, "Just look at that little Hasid!"

"Hey, you ninny, may an evil spirit possess your father's son!" one boy called out to me.

I left, laden with candy. Then I reached Krasinski Park. I was nearly run over while crossing the street. I entered the park and ate some of the delicacies. A boy passed by and I gave him a chocolate bar. Instead of saying thank you, he grabbed it and ran off. I walked over to the lake and fed the swans—with chocolate. Women pointed their fingers at me, laughed, made comments in Polish. Daintily dressed girls, with hoops and balls, came over to me and I chivalrously and prodigally distributed my candy among them. At that moment I felt like a rich nobleman distributing largess.

After a while I had no more candies, but I still had some money. I decided to take another droshky. When I sat in the second droshky and the driver asked where I wanted to go, I really wanted to say, "Krochmalna Street." But someone inside of me, an invisible glutton, answered instead, "To Marshalkovsky Boulevard."

"What number?"

I invented a number.

This coachman was honest. He took me to the address and did not ask for the money in advance. On the way another droshky rode alongside ours; inside sat a lady with an enormous bosom and a big hat decorated with an ostrich feather. My driver chatted with the other driver. Both spoke Yiddish, which the lady did not like at all. Even less did she like the little passenger with the black velvet hat and the red earlocks. She threw angry looks at me. From time to time both droshkies stopped to let a trolley car or a heavily laden wagon pass by. A policeman standing near the trolley tracks stared at me, at the lady, seemed for a minute about to come over and arrest me—and then began to laugh. I was terribly afraid. I was afraid of God, of my mother and father, and I was also afraid a hole had suddenly appeared in my pocket and my money had fallen through. And what if the driver was a robber carrying me off to some dark cave? Perhaps he was a magician. And perhaps all this was only a dream. But no, the driver was not a robber, and he did not carry me off to the twelve thieves in the desert. He took me exactly to the address I had given him, a big house with a gateway, and I paid him the forty groschen.

"Who are you going to see?" he asked me.

"A doctor," I answered without hesitation.

"What's the matter with you?"

"I cough."

"You're an orphan, eh?"

"Yes, an orphan."

"From out of town?"

"Yes."

"From where?"

I gave him the name of some town.

"Do you wear the fringed garment?"

This last question I did not answer. What concern of his were my ritual fringes? I wanted him to drive off, but he remained there with his droshky, and I could delay no longer—I had to enter the gateway. But behind the gate there lurked a gigantic dog. He looked at me with a pair of knowing eyes that seemed to say: "You may fool the coachman, but not me. I know you have no business here." And he opened a mouth full of sharp, pointed teeth.

Suddenly the janitor appeared. "And what do you want?"

I tried to stammer something, but he shouted at me, "Get away from here!"

And he began to chase me with a broom. I started to run, and the dog let out a savage howl. The droshky driver was probably a witness to my shame—but against a broom, a janitor, and a dog, a small boy cannot be a hero.

Things were not going well for me, but I still had some money left. And with money one can find pleasures anywhere. I saw a fruit store and went in. I ordered the first fruit I saw, and when it came to paying, my money was just barely enough. I parted with my last groschen.

I no longer remember what kind of fruit it was. It must have been a pomegranate or something equally exotic. I could not peel it, and when I ate it, it had a poisonous taste. Nevertheless I devoured it all. But then I was overcome by a horrible thirst. My throat was parched and burning. I had only one desire—to drink. Oh, if only I had money now! I could have emptied a gallon of soda water! But I had nothing and, furthermore, I was far from home.

I started to walk home. I walked and suddenly I felt a nail in my boot. It pierced my flesh at every step. How did the nail happen to be there just then? I stepped into a gateway. Here there were no dogs and no janitors. I took off the boot. Inside, right through the inner sole, a pointy nail was sticking up. I stuffed some paper into the boot and set out again. Oh, how bitter it is to walk when an iron nail pricks you at every step! And how bitter it must be to lie on a bed of nails in Gehenna! This day I had committed many sins. I had said no blessing before eating the candy, I had not given even one groschen of all my money to the poor. I had only gorged myself.

The walk home took about two hours. All manner of frightening thoughts beset me as I walked. Perhaps something terrible had happened at home. Perhaps I had not been lying when I told the coachman I was an orphan, but at the very moment when I said it I was in truth orphaned. Perhaps I had no father, no mother, no home. Perhaps my face had changed, like that of the man in the storybook, and when I got home Father and Mother would not recognize me. Anything was possible!

A boy saw me and stopped me. "Where are you coming from? Your mother has been looking for you everywhere!"

"I was in Praga—I rode on a trolley," I said, telling lies now just for the sake of lying. Because once you have eaten without a blessing and committed other sins, then you can do anything—it no longer matters.

"Who did you visit in Praga?"

"My aunt."

"Since when do you have an aunt in Praga?"

"She just came to Warsaw."

"Go on, you're fibbing. Your mother is looking for you. Swear you were in Praga."

I swore falsely too. Then I went home, tired, sweating—a lost soul. I pounced upon the water faucet and began to drink, to drink. Thus must Esau have devoured the mess of pottage for which he sold his birthright.

Mother wrung her hands. "Just look at that child!"

Why the Geese Shrieked

Selling geese

N our home there was always talk about spirits of the dead that possess the bodies of the living, souls reincarnated as animals, houses inhabited by hobgoblins, cellars haunted by demons. My father spoke of these things, first of all because he was interested in them, and second because in a big city children so easily go astray. They go everywhere, see everything, read non-religious books. It is necessary to remind them from time to time that there are still mysterious forces at work in the world.

One day, when I was about eight, he told us a story found in one of the holy books. If I am not mistaken, the author of that book is Rabbi Eliyahu Graidiker, or one of the other Graidiker sages. The story was about a girl possessed by four demons. It was said that they could actually be seen crawling around in her intestines, blowing up her belly, wandering from one part of her body to another, slithering into her legs. The Rabbi of Graidik had exorcised the evil spirits with the blowing of the ram's horn, with incantations, and the incense of magic herbs.

When my brother Joshua questioned these things, **39**

my father became very excited. He argued: "Was then the great Rabbi of Graidik, God forbid, a liar? Are all the rabbis, saints, and sages deceivers, while only atheists speak the truth? Woe is us! How can one be so blind?"

Suddenly the door opened, and a woman entered. She was carrying a basket with two geese in it. The woman looked frightened. Her matron's wig was tilted to one side. She smiled nervously.

Father never looked at strange women, because it is forbidden by Jewish law, but Mother and we children saw immediately that something had greatly upset our unexpected visitor.

"What is it?" Father asked, at the same time turning his back so as not to look upon her.

"Rabbi, I have a very unusual problem."

"What is it?"

"It's about these geese."

"What's the matter with them?"

"Dear Rabbi, the geese were slaughtered properly. Then I cut off their heads. I took out the intestines, the livers, all the other organs, but the geese keep shrieking in such a sorrowful voice . . ."

Upon hearing these words, my father turned pale. A dreadful fear befell me, too. But my mother came from a family of rationalists and was by nature a skeptic.

"Slaughtered geese don't shriek," she said.

"You will hear for yourself," replied the woman.

She took one of the geese and placed it on the table. 40 Then she took out the second goose. The geese were headless, disemboweled—in short, ordinary dead geese.

A smile appeared on my mother's lips. "And *these* geese shriek?"

"You will soon hear."

The woman took one goose and hurled it against the other. At once a shriek was heard. It is not easy to describe that sound. It was like the cackling of a goose, but in such a high, eerie pitch, with such groaning and quaking, that my limbs grew cold. I could actually feel the hairs of my earlocks pricking me. I wanted to run from the room. But where would I run? My throat constricted with fear. Then I, too, shrieked and clung to my mother's skirt, like a child of three.

Father forgot that one must avert one's eyes from a woman. He ran to the table. He was no less frightened than I was. His red beard trembled. In his blue eyes could be seen a mixture of fear and vindication. For my father this was a sign that not only to the Rabbi of Graidik, but to him too, omens were sent from heaven. But perhaps this was a sign from the Evil One, from Satan himself?

"What do you say now?" asked the woman.

My mother was no longer smiling. In her eyes there was something like sadness, and also anger.

"I cannot understand what is going on here," she said, with a certain resentment.

"Do you want to hear it again?"

Again the woman threw one goose against the other. And again the dead geese gave forth an uncanny shriek—the shriek of dumb creatures slain by the *41* slaughterer's knife who yet retain a living force; who still have a reckoning to make with the living, an injustice to avenge. A chill crept over me. I felt as though someone had struck me with all his might.

My father's voice became hoarse. It was broken as though by sobs. "Well, can anyone still doubt that there *is* a Creator?" he asked.

"Rabbi, what shall I do and where shall I go?" The woman began to croon in a mournful singsong. "What has befallen me? Woe is me! What shall I do with them? Perhaps I should run to one of the Wonder Rabbis? Perhaps they were not slaughtered properly? I am afraid to take them home. I wanted to prepare them for the Sabbath meal, and now, such a calamity! Holy Rabbi, what shall I do? Must I throw them out? Someone said they must be wrapped in shrouds and buried in a grave. I am a poor woman. Two geese! They cost me a fortune!"

Father did not know what to answer. He glanced at his bookcase. If there was an answer anywhere, it must be there.

Suddenly he looked angrily at my mother. "And what do you say now, eh?"

Mother's face was growing sullen, smaller, sharper. In her eyes could be seen indignation and also something like shame.

"I want to hear it again." Her words were half pleading, half commanding.

The woman hurled the geese against each other for the third time, and for the third time the shrieks were heard. It occurred to me that such must have been the voice of the sacrificial heifer.

"Woe, woe, and still they blaspheme . . . It is written that the wicked do not repent even at the very gates of hell." Father had again begun to speak. "They behold the truth with their own eyes, and they continue to deny their Maker. They are dragged into the bottomless pit and they maintain that all is nature, or accident . . ."

He looked at Mother as if to say: You take after *them*.

For a long time there was silence. Then the woman asked, "Well, did I just imagine it?"

Suddenly my mother laughed. There was something in her laughter that made us all tremble. I knew, by some sixth sense, that Mother was preparing to end the mighty drama being enacted before our eyes.

"Did you remove the windpipes?" my mother asked.

"The windpipes? No . . ."

"Take them out," said my mother, "and the geese will stop shrieking."

My father became angry. "What are you babbling? What has this got to do with windpipes?"

Mother took hold of one of the geese, pushed her slender finger inside the body, and with all her might pulled out the thin tube that led from the neck to the lungs. Then she took the other goose and removed its windpipe also. I stood trembling, aghast at my mother's courage. Her hands had become bloodied. On her face could be seen the wrath of the rationalist whom someone has tried to frighten in broad daylight.

Father's face turned white, calm, a little disappointed. He knew what had happened here: logic, cold logic, was again tearing down faith, mocking it, holding it up to ridicule and scorn.

"Now, if you please, take one goose and hurl it against the other!" commanded my mother.

Everything hung in the balance. If the geese shrieked, Mother would have lost all: her rationalist's daring, her skepticism, which she had inherited from her intellectual father. And I? Although I was afraid, I prayed inwardly that the geese *would* shriek, shriek so loud that people in the street would hear and come running.

But, alas, the geese were silent, silent as only two dead geese without windpipes can be.

"Bring me a towel!" Mother turned to me.

I ran to get the towel. There were tears in my eyes. Mother wiped her hands on the towel like a surgeon after a difficult operation.

"That's all it was!" she announced victoriously.

"Rabbi, what do you say?" asked the woman.

Father began to cough, to mumble. He fanned himself with his skullcap.

"I have never before heard of such a thing," he said at last.

"Nor have I," echoed the woman.

"Nor have I," said my mother. "But there is always an explanation. Dead geese don't shriek."

"Can I go home now and cook them?" asked the woman.

"Go home and cook them for the Sabbath." Mother pronounced the decision. "Don't be afraid. They won't make a sound in your pot."

"What do you say, Rabbi?"

"Hmm . . . they are kosher," murmured Father. "They can be eaten." He was not really convinced, but now he could not pronounce the geese unclean.

Mother went back to the kitchen. I remained with my father. Suddenly he began to speak to me as though I were an adult. "Your mother takes after your grandfather, the Rabbi of Bilgoray. He is a great scholar, but a cold-blooded rationalist. People warned me before our betrothal . . ."

And then Father threw up his hands, as if to say: It is too late now to call off the wedding.

Reb Asher the Dairyman

Jewish boys of Warsaw

HERE are some people in this world who are simply born good. Such was Reb Asher the dairyman. God had endowed him with many, many gifts. He was tall, broad, strong, had a black beard, large black eyes, and the voice of a lion. On the New Year and the Day of Atonement he served as cantor of the main prayer for the congregation that met in our house, and it was his voice that attracted many of the worshippers. He did this without payment, although he could have commanded sizable fees from some of the larger synagogues. It was his way of helping my father earn a livelihood for the holidays. And as if this were not enough, Reb Asher was always doing something for us in one way or another. No one sent my father as generous a Purim gift as did Reb Asher the dairyman. When Father found himself in great straits and could not pay the rent, he sent me to Reb Asher to borrow the money. And Asher never said no, nor did he ever pull a wry face. He simply reached into his pants pocket and pulled out a handful of paper money and silver. Neither did he limit himself to helping out my father. He gave charity in all directions. This simple

51

Jew, who with great difficulty plowed through a chapter of the Mishnah, lived his entire life on the highest ethical plane. What others preached, he practiced.

He was no millionaire, he was not even wealthy, but he had a "comfortable income," as my father would put it. I myself often bought milk, butter, cheese, clabber, and cream in his shop. His wife and their eldest daughter waited on customers all day long, from early in the morning till late at night. His wife was a stout woman, with a blond wig, puffy cheeks, and a neck covered with freckles. She was the daughter of a farm bailiff. Her enormous bosom seemed to be swollen with milk. I used to imagine that if someone were to cut her arm, milk would spurt out, not blood. One son, Yudl, was so fat that people came to stare at him as at a freak. He weighed nearly three hundred and fifty pounds. Another son, slight of build and something of a dandy, had become a tailor and gone off to Paris. A younger son was still studying at cheder, and a little girl attended a secular school.

Just as our house was always filled with problems, doubts, and unrest, so everything in Asher's house was whole, placid, healthy. Every day Asher went to bring the cans of milk from the train. He rose at dawn, went to the synagogue, and after breakfast drove to the railroad depot. He worked at least eighteen hours every day, yet on the Sabbath, instead of resting, he would go to listen to a preacher or come to my father to study a portion of the Pentateuch with the commentary of Rashi. Just as he loved his work, so he loved his Judaism. It seems to me that I never heard this man say no. His entire life was one great yes.

Asher owned a horse and wagon, and this horse and wagon aroused a fierce envy in me. How happy must be the boy whose father owned a wagon, a horse, a stable! Every day Asher went off to distant parts of the city, even to Praga! Often I would see him driving past our building. He never forgot to lift his head and greet whomever he saw at the window or on the balcony. Often he met me when I was running about the streets with a gang of boys or playing with those who were not "my kind," but he never threatened to tell my father, nor did he try to lecture me. He did not, like the other grown-ups, pull little boys by the ear, pinch their noses, or twist the brims of their caps. Asher seemed to have an innate respect for every one, big or small.

Once when I saw him driving by in his wagon I nodded to him and called out, "Reb Asher, take me along!"

Asher immediately stopped and told me to get on. We drove to a train depot. The trip took several hours and I was overjoyed. I rode amid trolley cars, droshkies, delivery vans. Soldiers marched; policemen stood guard; fire engines, ambulances, even some of the automobiles that were just beginning to appear on the streets of Warsaw rushed past us. Nothing could harm me. I was protected by a friend with a whip, and beneath my feet I could feel the throbbing of the wheels. It seemed to me that all Warsaw must envy me. And indeed people stared in wonderment at the little Hasid with the velvet cap and the red earlocks who was riding in a milk wagon and surveying the city. It was evident that I did not really belong to this wagon, that I was a strange kind of tourist . . .

From that day on, a silent pact existed between me and Reb Asher. Whenever he could, he would take me along as his passenger. Fraught with danger were those minutes when Reb Asher went off to fetch the milk cans from the train, or to attend to a bill, and I remained alone in the wagon. The horse would turn his head and stare at me in astonishment. Asher had given me the reins to hold, and the horse seemed to be saying silently, "Just look who is my driver now . . ." The fear that the horse might suddenly rear up and run off gave to these moments the extra fillip of peril. After all, a horse is not a child's plaything but a gigantic creature, silent, wild, with enormous strength. Occasionally a Gentile would pass by, look at me, laugh, and say something to me in Polish. I did not understand his language, and he cast the same sort of dread upon me as did the horse: he too was big, strong, and incomprehensible. He too might suddenly turn on me and strike me, or yank at my earlock—a pastime some Poles considered a great joke . . .

When I thought the end had come—any moment now the Gentile would strike me, or the horse would dash off and smash into a wall or a street lamp—then Reb Asher reappeared and all was well again. Asher carried the heavy milk cans with the ease of a Samson. He was stronger than the horse, stronger than the Gentile, yet he had mild eyes and spoke my language, and he was my father's friend. I had only one desire: to ride with this man for days and nights over fields and through forests, to Africa, to America, to the ends of the world, and always to watch, to observe all that was going on around me . . .

How different this same Asher seemed on the New Year and the Day of Atonement! Carpenters had put up benches in my father's study, and this was where the women prayed. The beds had been taken out of the bedroom, a Holy Ark brought in, and it had become a tiny prayer house. Asher was dressed in a white robe, against which his black beard appeared even blacker. On his head he wore a high cap embroidered with gold and silver. At the beginning of the Additional Service, Reb Asher would ascend to the cantor's desk and recite in a lion's roar: "Behold me, destitute of good works . . ."

Our bedroom was too small for the bass voice that thundered forth from this mighty breast. It was heard halfway down the street. Asher recited and chanted. He knew every melody, every movement. The twenty men who made up our congregation were all part of his choir. Asher's deep masculine voice aroused a tumult in the women's section. True, they all knew him well. Only yesterday they had bought from him or from his wife a saucepan of milk, a pot of clabber, a few ounces of butter, and had bargained with him for a little extra. But now Asher was the delegate who offered up the prayers of the People of Israel directly to the Almighty, before the Throne of Glory, amid fluttering angels and books that read

55

themselves, in which are recorded the good deeds and the sins of every mortal soul . . . When he reached the prayer "We will express the might," and began to recite the destinies of men—who shall live and who shall die, who shall perish by fire and who by water —a sobbing broke out among the women. But when Asher called out triumphantly: "But repentance, prayer, and charity can avert the evil decree!"—then a heavy stone was taken from every heart. Soon Asher began to sing of the smallness of man and the greatness of God, and joy and comfort enveloped everyone. Why need men—who are but passing shadows, wilting blossoms—expect malice from a God who is just, revered, merciful? Every word that Asher called out, every note he uttered, restored courage, revived hope. We indeed are nothing, but He is all. We are but as dust in our lifetime, and less than dust after death, but He is eternal and His days shall never end. In Him, only in Him, lies our hope . . .

One year, at the close of the Day of Atonement, this same Asher, our friend and benefactor, saved our very lives. It happened in this way. After the day-long fast, we had eaten a rich supper. Later a number of Jews gathered in our house to dance and rejoice. My father had already put up, in the courtyard, the first beam of the hut for the coming Feast of Tabernacles. Late that night the family had at last fallen asleep. Since benches and pews had been set up in the bedroom, and the entire house was in disorder, each of us slept wherever he could find a spot. But one thing we had forgotten—to extinguish the candles that were still burning on some of the pews.

Late that night Asher had to drive to the railroad station to pick up milk. He passed our building and noticed that our apartment was unusually bright. This was not the glow of candles or a lamp, but the glare of a fire. Asher realized that our house must be burning. He rang the bell at the gate but the janitor did not rush to open it. He too was asleep. Then Asher set to ringing the bell and beating on the door, making such a commotion that at last the janitor awoke and opened the gate. Asher raced up the stairs and banged on our door, but no one answered. Then Asher the Mighty hurled his broad shoulders against the door and forced it open. Bursting into the apartment, he found the entire family asleep, while all around benches, prayer stands, and prayer books were aflame. He began to shout in his booming cantorial voice and finally roused us, and then he tore off our quilts and set to smothering the conflagration.

I remember that moment as though it was yesterday. I opened my eyes and saw many flames, large and small, rolling about and dancing like imps. My brother Moshe's blanket had already caught fire. But I was young and was not frightened. On the contrary, I liked the dancing flames.

After some time the fire was put out. Here indeed something had happened that might well be called a miracle. A few minutes more, and we all would have been taken by the flames, for the wood of the benches was dry and they were saturated with the tallow of the dripping candles. Asher was the only human being awake at that hour, the only one who would ring the bell so persistently and risk his own life for us. Yes, it was fated that this faithful friend should save us from the fire.

We were not even able to thank him. It was as though we had all been struck dumb. Asher himself was in a hurry and left quickly. We wandered about amid the charred benches, tables, prayer books, and prayer shawls, and every few minutes we discovered more sparks and smoldering embers. We all might easily have been burned to cinders.

The friendship between my father and Reb Asher grew ever stronger, and during the war years, when we were close to starvation, Asher again helped us in every way he could.

After we had left Warsaw (during the First World War), we continued to hear news of him from time to time. One son died, a daughter fell in love with a young man of low origins and Asher was deeply grieved. I do not know whether he lived to see the Nazi occupation of Warsaw. He probably died before that. But such Jews as he were dragged off to the death camps. May these memoirs serve as a monument to him and his like, who lived in sanctity and died as martyrs.

To the Wild Cows

At the market: a fruit and vegetable stall

N all the years that we lived in Warsaw, I never left the city. Other boys used to talk about their vacations. People went out to Falenica, to Miedzeszyn, Michalin, Swider, Otwock—but for me these were only names. No trees grew on Krochmalna Street. Near No. 24, where I went to cheder, there was a tree, but No. 24 was far from our house.

Some of the neighbors had potted flowers, but my parents considered this a pagan custom. I, however, had an inborn love of nature. In the summertime I would sometimes find a leaf still attached to the stem of an apple, and such a leaf would arouse both joy and longing in me. I would sniff at it and carry it around with me until it withered. Mother brought home a bunch of carrots, parsley, red radishes, cucumbers—and every vegetable reminded me of the days in Radzymin, where I had been surrounded by fields and orchards. Once I found a whole ear of corn in my straw mattress. This ear of corn awakened many memories. Among other things it reminded me of the dream of Pharaoh, wherein the seven lean ears of corn devoured the seven fat ones.

63

Many different kinds of flies used to alight on the railing of our balcony : large, small, dark, green-gold. When a butterfly would stray there, I would not try to catch it, but would hold my breath and stare in wonder. The little fluttering creature was for me a greeting from the world of freedom.

But Mother Nature did her work even on Krochmalna Street. In the winter the snow fell, in the summer the rains came. High over the rooftops the clouds passed—dark ones, light ones, some like silver, some in the shapes of fish, snakes, sheep, brooms. Occasionally hail fell on our balcony, and once, after the rain, a rainbow stretched above the roofs. Father told me to recite the blessing "Who remembereth the Covenant." At night the moon shone and the stars appeared. It was all a great mystery.

My friend Boruch-Dovid was always talking about the fields and wastelands that lie beyond Warsaw, and about the wild cows that graze there. I began to demand that he take me there. He delayed as long as he could and put me off with various excuses. But finally it reached the point where he had to make good on his promises or our friendship would end.

One Friday in the summertime I arose very early, so early that the sky was still glowing from the sunrise. To my mother I made some pretext or other, put a few slices of bread and butter in a paper bag, took from its hiding place a kopeck I had somehow saved from my allowance, and went off to meet Boruch-Dovid. I had never been up so early in the morning, and everything looked cooler, fresher, and somehow like a fairy-tale landscape. Here and there a stone was damp and Boruch-Dovid said it was because of the dew. This meant, then, that there was dew even on Krochmalna Street. I had thought that dew fell only in the Land of Israel . . .

Not only the street, but the people too looked fresher. I discovered that early in the morning various farm wagons came to our street. Gentiles from the surrounding villages brought vegetables, chickens, geese, ducks, and freshly laid chicken eggs (not the lime-preserved eggs one could buy in Zelda's shop). On Mirowski Street, behind the market halls, was the wholesale fruit market. The abundance of all the orchards around Warsaw was brought here: apples, pears, cherries, sour cherries, gooseberries, currants. Here too were traded strange fruits and vegetables that most Jewish children had never tasted and thought forbidden: tomatoes, cauliflowers, green peppers. Inside the market halls proper, one could get pomegranates and bananas. These were bought only by grand ladies, whose shopping baskets were carried by servant girls.

Boruch-Dovid and I walked quickly. As we walked, he told many strange tales. His father, he said, had gone on foot from Warsaw to Skierniewice and on the way he had met a wild man. I was very curious about the appearance of the wild man and Boruch-Dovid gave me a detailed description: tall, with scales instead of skin, long hair reaching to the ground, and a horn growing in the middle of his forehead. For breakfast such a creature always ate a live child. I was panic-stricken and I asked, "Maybe a wild man will attack us?"

"No, they are far from Warsaw."

I should not have been so gullible. But I always believed everything Boruch-Dovid told me.

We passed through Nalewki and Muranow Streets, and from there the road led to the open country. I saw broad meadows covered with grass and all sorts of flowers, and mountains of a kind I had never known to exist. At the top they were indeed mountains, but at the bottom there were brick walls with small, sunken windows covered by iron grates.

"What is that?" I asked.

"The Citadel."

A feeling of dread came over me. I had heard of the Citadel. Here were imprisoned those who had tried to overthrow the Tsar.

I had not yet seen any wild cows, but what I had seen already was wonderful and strange. The sky here was not a narrow strip as on Krochmalna Street, but broad, spread out like the ocean, and it descended to the earth like a heavenly curtain. Birds flew overhead in swarms, with a twittering, a cawing, a whistling—large birds and small birds. Two storks were circling above one of the hills of the Citadel. Butterflies of all colors fluttered above the grass : white, yellow, brown, with all kinds of dots and patterns. The air smelled of earth, of grass, of the smoke of locomotives, and of something more that intoxicated me and made my head reel. There was a strange stillness here, and yet everything murmured, rustled, chirped. Blossoms fell from somewhere and settled on the lapels of my coat. I looked up at the sky, saw the sun, the clouds, and suddenly I understood more clearly the meaning of the words of Genesis. This, then, was the world God had created: the earth, the heavens, the waters above that are separated by the firmament from the waters below.

Boruch-Dovid and I climbed up a hill and below us we saw the Vistula. One half glittered like silver, the other half was green as gall. A white ship sailed past. The river itself did not stand still—it flowed, it was headed somewhere, with an eagerness that hinted at miracles and the coming of the Messiah.

"That's the Vistula," explained Boruch-Dovid. "It flows all the way to Danzig."

"And then?"

"Then it flows into the sea."

"And where is the Leviathan?"

"Far away, at the end of the earth."

Then the storybooks did not tell lies, after all. The world *is* filled with wonders. One need merely pass through Muranow Street and one street more, and already one was in the midst of marvels. The end of the earth? Was not *this* the end of the earth? . . .

Locomotives whistled, but no trains could be seen. Gentle breezes were blowing, and each brought with it a different fragrance—aromas long forgotten or never dreamed of. A honeybee came from somewhere, alit on a flower, smelled at it, hummed, and flew on to the next flower. Boruch-Dovid said, "She wants to collect honey."

"Can she bite?"

"Yes, and she has a special poison."

He, Boruch-Dovid, knows everything. If I were alone, I could not find my way home. Already I have forgotten even the direction toward Warsaw. But he is as much at home here as in his own courtyard. Suddenly he starts to run. He pretends to run away from me. He throws himself down and is hidden by the tall grass. Boruch-Dovid is gone! I am alone in the world—a lost child, just like in the storybooks.

"Boruch-Dovid!" I began to call. "Boruch-Dovid!"

I call, but my voice rebounds from somewhere. There is an echo here, as in a synagogue, but it is thrown back from a great distance and the voice is changed and terrifying.

"Boruch-Dovid! Boruch-Dovid! . . ."

I know that he is only playing a joke on me. He wants to frighten me. But though I know it, I am afraid. My voice is breaking with sobs.

"Bo-r-uch Do-v-id! . . ."

He reappears, his black eyes laughing like a gypsy's, and begins to run about in circles like a young colt. His coattails fly. His fringed vest billows in the wind. He too has become like a wild creature in the lap of nature.

"Come on, let's go to the Vistula!"

The path leads downhill, and we cannot walk—we run. Our feet seem to be running by themselves. I have to hold mine back so they won't run even faster and jump right into the water. But the water is farther away than I had thought. As I run, the river becomes broader, like an ocean. We come to dunes of pebbles and moist sand, long and marked with lines, like giant cakes made by children playing in the sand. Boruch-Dovid takes off his boots, rolls up his pants legs, and wades into the water up to his ankles.

"Ouch, it's cold!"

He tells me to take off my boots. But I am embarrassed. Walking barefoot is not in my nature. Only rowdies and Gentile boys go barefoot.

"Are there any fish here?"

"Yes, lots of fish."

"Do they bite?"

"Sometimes."

"What will you do if a fish bites you?"

"I'll grab it by the tail . . ."

Compared to me, Boruch-Dovid is a country boy, a peasant. I sit down on a rock and everything inside me flows, gurgles like the waters of the Vistula. My mind sways with the motion of the waves and it seems to me that not only the Vistula, but everything around me—the hills, the sky, I myself—is swaying, flowing away into the distance, toward Danzig. Boruch-Dovid points to the other shore and says, "Over there is the Praga forest."

This means that near me there is a real forest, full of wild animals and robbers.

Suddenly something extraordinary happens. From the left, where the sky and the waters meet, something comes floating on the water, but it is not a ship. At first it seems small, enveloped in a haze. Soon it grows larger and more distinct. It is a group of rafts made of logs. Men lean against long poles and push them with all the weight of their bodies. On one of the rafts there is a little hut—a small house out on the water! Even Boruch-Dovid stares in open-mouthed wonder.

It takes a long, long time for the rafts to come close to us. The men yell something to us. I notice someone who looks like a Jew. He has a beard. I think I can even make out a Jewish skullcap. From my reading of the parables of the Preacher of Dubnow, I know that Jewish merchants make voyages to Danzig and Leipzig. I have even heard that timber is shipped by water. But now I see it with my own eyes—a tale of the Dubnow preacher brought to life! For a while the rafts are near us. A dog stands at the edge of one of them and barks directly at us. Woe to us, if he could jump across the water! He would tear us to shreds. After a while, the rafts move on. Time has passed, the sun has already reached the middle of the sky and is now moving into the West. Only after the rafts have disappeared beneath a bridge do we start to go back, not the way we came, but in a different direction.

I remember the wild cows and am about to ask Boruch-Dovid where they are, but I don't. I suddenly realize that the wild cows and the wild man are nothing but his imagination. We would never encounter any of them. As a matter of fact, when I had told my mother about the wild cows, she had asked, "If there are such cows, why don't they catch them and sell them to the dairies? And how is it possible that they have only been seen by your friend Boruch-Dovid?" She was just as skeptical about the wild cows as she had been about the shrieking geese.

The sun is reddening. At home Mother is surely beginning to worry—she is so nervous. Soon it will be time to take the Sabbath stew to the baker, and who will be there to carry it? We begin to walk quickly, each sunk in his own thoughts, while above our heads the birds play, and the windows of the Citadel glow red and gold in the sunset.

I think of those who lie inside in chains because they tried to overthrow the Tsar. I seem to see their eyes, and suddenly everything is filled with a Sabbath Eve sadness and eeriness.

The Washwoman

A family of bagel peddlers

OUR home had little contact with Gentiles. The only Gentile in the building was the janitor. Fridays he would come for a tip, his "Friday money." He remained standing at the door, took off his hat, and my mother gave him six groschen.

Besides the janitor there were also the Gentile washwomen who came to the house to fetch our laundry. My story is about one of these.

She was a small woman, old and wrinkled. When she started washing for us, she was already past seventy. Most Jewish women of her age were sickly, weak, broken in body. All the old women in our street had bent backs and leaned on sticks when they walked. But this washwoman, small and thin as she was, possessed a strength that came from generations of peasant forebears. Mother would count out to her a bundle of laundry that had accumulated over several weeks. She would lift the unwieldy pack, load it on her narrow shoulders, and carry it the long way home. She lived on Krochmalna Street too, but at the other end, near the Wola section. It must have been a walk of an hour and a half.

She would bring the laundry back about two weeks later. My mother had never been so pleased with any washwoman. Every piece of linen sparkled like polished silver. Every piece was neatly ironed. Yet she charged no more than the others. She was a real find. Mother always had her money ready, because it was too far for the old woman to come a second time.

Laundering was not easy in those days. The old woman had no faucet where she lived but had to bring in the water from a pump. For the linens to come out so clean, they had to be scrubbed thoroughly in a washtub, rinsed with washing soda, soaked, boiled in an enormous pot, starched, then ironed. Every piece was handled ten times or more. And the drying! It could not be done outside because thieves would steal the laundry. The wrung-out wash had to be carried up to the attic and hung on clotheslines. In the winter it would become as brittle as glass and almost break when touched. And there was always a to-do with other housewives and washwomen who wanted the attic clotheslines for their own use. Only God knows all the old woman had to endure each time she did a wash!

She could have begged at the church door or entered a home for the penniless and aged. But there was in her a certain pride and love of labor with which many Gentiles have been blessed. The old woman did not want to become a burden, and so she bore her burden.

My mother spoke a little Polish, and the old woman would talk with her about many things. She was especially fond of me and used to say I looked like

Jesus. She repeated this every time she came, and Mother would frown and whisper to herself, her lips barely moving, "May her words be scattered in the wilderness."

The woman had a son who was rich. I no longer remember what sort of business he had. He was ashamed of his mother, the washwoman, and never came to see her. Nor did he ever give her a groschen. The old woman told this without rancor. One day the son was married. It seemed that he had made a good match. The wedding took place in a church. The son had not invited the old mother to his wedding, but she went to the church and waited at the steps to see her son lead the "young lady" to the altar.

The story of the faithless son left a deep impression on my mother. She talked about it for weeks and months. It was an affront not only to the old woman but to the entire institution of motherhood. Mother would argue, "Nu, does it pay to make sacrifices for children? The mother uses up her last strength, and he does not even know the meaning of loyalty."

And she would drop dark hints to the effect that she was not certain of her own children: Who knows what they would do some day? This, however, did not prevent her from dedicating her life to us. If there was any delicacy in the house, she would put it aside for the children and invent all sorts of excuses and reasons why she herself did not want to taste it. She knew charms that went back to ancient times, and she used expressions she had inherited from generations of devoted mothers and grandmothers. If one of the children complained of a pain, she would say, "May I be your ransom and may you outlive my bones!" Or she would say, "May I be the atonement for the least of your fingernails." When we ate she used to say, "Health and marrow in your bones!" The day before the new moon she gave us a kind of candy that was said to prevent parasitic worms. If one of us had something in his eye, Mother would lick the eye clean with her tongue. She also fed us rock candy against coughs, and from time to time she would take us to be blessed against the evil eye. This did not prevent her from studying *The Duties of the Heart*, *The Book of the Covenant*, and other serious philosophic works.

But to return to the washwoman. That winter was a harsh one. The streets were in the grip of a bitter cold. No matter how much we heated our stove, the windows were covered with frostwork and decorated with icicles. The newspapers reported that people were dying of the cold. Coal became dear. The winter had become so severe that parents stopped sending children to cheder, and even the Polish schools were closed.

On one such day the washwoman, now nearly eighty years old, came to our house. A good deal of laundry had accumulated during the past weeks. Mother gave her a pot of tea to warm herself, as well as some bread. The old woman sat on a kitchen chair trembling and shaking, and warmed her hands against the teapot. Her fingers were gnarled from work, and perhaps from arthritis too. Her fingernails were strangely white. These hands spoke of the stubbornness of mankind, of the will to work not only as one's strength permits but beyond the limits of one's power. Mother counted and wrote down the list: men's undershirts, women's vests, long-legged drawers, bloomers, petticoats, shifts, featherbed covers, pillowcases, sheets, and the men's fringed garments. Yes, the Gentile woman washed these holy garments as well.

The bundle was big, bigger than usual. When the woman placed it on her shoulders, it covered her completely. At first she swayed, as though she were about to fall under the load. But an inner obstinacy seemed to call out: No, you may not fall. A donkey may permit himself to fall under his burden, but not a human being, the crown of creation.

It was fearful to watch the old woman staggering out with the enormous pack, out into the frost, where the snow was dry as salt and the air was filled with dusty white whirlwinds, like goblins dancing in the cold. Would the old woman ever reach Wola?

She disappeared, and Mother sighed and prayed for her.

Usually the woman brought back the wash after two or, at the most, three weeks. But three weeks passed, then four and five, and nothing was heard of the old woman. We remained without linens. The cold had become even more intense. The telephone wires were now as thick as ropes. The branches of the trees looked like glass. So much snow had fallen that the streets had become uneven, and sleds were able to glide down many streets as on the slopes of a hill. Kindhearted people lit fires in the streets for vagrants to warm themselves and roast potatoes in, if they had any to roast.

For us the washwoman's absence was a catastrophe. We needed the laundry. We did not even know the woman's address. It seemed certain that she had collapsed, died. Mother declared she had had a premonition, as the old woman left our house that last time, that we would never see our things again. She found some old torn shirts and washed and mended them. We mourned, both for the laundry and for the old, toil-worn woman who had grown close to us through the years she had served us so faithfully.

More than two months passed. The frost had subsided, and then a new frost had come, a new wave of cold. One evening, while Mother was sitting near the kerosene lamp mending a shirt, the door opened and a small puff of steam, followed by a gigantic bundle, entered. Under the bundle tottered the old woman, her face as white as a linen sheet. A few wisps of white hair straggled out from beneath her shawl. Mother uttered a half-choked cry. It was as though a corpse had entered the room. I ran toward the old woman and helped her unload her pack. She was even thinner now, more bent. Her face had become more gaunt, and her head shook from side to side as though she were saying no. She could not utter a clear word, but mumbled something with her sunken mouth and pale lips.

After the old woman had recovered somewhat, she told us that she had been ill, very ill. Just what her illness was, I cannot remember. She had been so sick that someone had called a doctor, and the doctor had sent for a priest. Someone had informed the son, and he had contributed money for a coffin and for the funeral. But the Almighty had not yet wanted to take this pain-racked soul to Himself. She began to feel better, she became well, and as soon as she was able to stand on her feet once more, she resumed her washing. Not just ours, but the wash of several other families too.

"I could not rest easy in my bed because of the wash," the old woman explained. "The wash would not let me die."

"With the help of God you will live to be a hundred and twenty," said my mother, as a benediction.

"God forbid! What good would such a long life be? The work becomes harder and harder . . . my strength is leaving me . . . I do not want to be a burden on anyone!" The old woman muttered and crossed herself, and raised her eyes toward heaven.

Fortunately there was some money in the house and Mother counted out what she owed. I had a strange feeling: the coins in the old woman's washed-out hands seemed to become as worn and clean and pious as she herself was. She blew on the coins and tied them in a kerchief. Then she left, promising to return in a few weeks for a new load of wash.

But she never came back. The wash she had returned was her last effort on this earth. She had been driven by an indomitable will to return the property to its rightful owners, to fulfill the task she had undertaken.

And now at last her body, which had long been no

more than a shard supported only by the force of honesty and duty, had fallen. Her soul passed into those spheres where all holy souls meet, regardless of the roles they played on this earth, in whatever tongue, of whatever creed. I cannot imagine paradise without this Gentile washwoman. I cannot even conceive of a world where there is no recompense for such effort.

I Become a Collector

In the one-room apartment of a metal worker

A RABBI like my father was supported by the people of his neighborhood. In need of his advice on matters of religious law, and knowing that he had to earn a living, they gave various sums each week to his collector. True, the collector made out receipts, but it was an easy matter for him to keep more than the 20 percent commission that was his due.

Our first collector was an honest man, but he later married and became a ritual slaughterer. Each of those who followed was more of a thief than the last, and by the time I was nine we had a collector who was taking most of the money for himself. Every week he would turn in less and less, with complaints: "I can't get them to pay!" or "There's a shortage, a crisis!" It was beneath my father's dignity to suspect another Jew.

Finally there wasn't a piece of bread in the house, and the storekeepers refused us credit. I no longer received a daily two-groschen piece for candy or chocolate. We could not pay the rent and the landlord threatened to take us to court and auction our furniture. When Father recited grace—"And let us not partake of the gifts of flesh and blood"—he would look

89

heavenward, sighing more deeply than usual. Was it possible to study the Torah and be a Jew if there was no Sabbath food?

One day when Father had been telling me his troubles, I said, "Let me collect!"

Stunned, Father looked at me. "But you're only a boy. You have to study."

"I'll study."

"What do you think Mother would say?"

"Why tell her?"

After deliberating awhile, he said, "Well, we'll try it."

I took the collection tickets to the necessary addresses, and in spite of the excuses made by my corrupt predecessor, donations were generous. Since we had discharged the collector several weeks before, many people were behind in their payments and within an hour my gaberdine pockets were full of copper and silver coins. In two hours, finding that both pockets were full, I began stuffing my breast pocket and my pants.

The shame I had felt diminished. Everyone was so gracious, the men pinching my cheeks, the women blessing me and treating me to cookies, fruit, and candy. My father, they told me, was a godly man, a saint. I kept climbing stairs, knocking at doors. Krochmalna Street, which I had thought I knew, was now turning itself inside out for me. I found tailors, cobblers, furriers, brushmakers, numerous artisans. In one apartment, girls were stringing coral, and colorful beads gleamed in piles on tables, chairs, and beds. It looked like an enchanted palace to me.

But when I opened the door of another apartment, I screamed. Dead animals were heaped on the floor. This tenant bought hares from a hunter and sold them to restaurants. In another apartment, girls were winding thread from spindles to bobbins, singing Yiddish songs while bits of thread flew into their disheveled hair.

In one place, people were playing cards, and in another an aged, white-bearded man planed a board while shavings and chips fell everywhere and a bonneted old woman prayed from a holy book. In a bookbinder's apartment I was horrified to find workers tramping over Pentateuchs and other holy books. Then in another apartment I found a female freak with a head that came almost to a point. She had huge calf's eyes and an extraordinarily broad body, and she grunted like a mute and made frightening sounds. Much to my surprise, I found that she had a husband.

Somewhere else I saw a sallow-faced, paralyzed man lying on a kind of shelf while a woman fed him and the food dribbled over his withered beard. His eyes seemed crossed. I shut that door almost as soon as I opened it. Up an incredibly filthy stairway I climbed to an attic, past barefoot, scurvy children playing with shards and mud. One boy's skull had been shaved. He was pale, his ears were swollen, and he had long, unkempt sidelocks. A girl spat at him and he cried out some kind of curse. Taking out a ticket, I asked, "Where does Yenta Flederbaum live?"

"In the *shtchonka* . . ."

In Warsaw this was the name for a dark hallway. I was inclined to be fearful, but that day I was somehow infused with great courage, as if I had been transformed. Stumbling along the dark corridor, bumping into baskets and crates, I heard a rustling noise, as if mice were about. Lighting a match, I discovered that there were no numbers or even latches on the doors. When I pushed one open, I was transfixed by what I saw. A corpse wrapped in a sheet lay on the floor, a pair of candles at its head and a woman beside it on a footstool, weeping, wringing her hands, and crying out. The mirror on the opposite wall had been draped. My ribs tingling with fright, I slammed the door and backed into the hallway, fiery spots before my eyes, my ears throbbing. I began to run but became entangled in a basket or crate. It was as if someone had clutched my coattail, drawing me backward; bony fingers dug into me, I heard a dreadful scream. In a cold sweat, I ran, tearing my gaberdine. There would be no more collecting for me. I threw up, and shivered. The coins burdened me as I walked. It seemed to me that I had grown old in that one day.

I had no appetite, even though I hadn't eaten since morning. My stomach felt swollen. I went into the Radzymin study house, where the men in our family prayed, and found it deserted because it was midday. Like an old man, I sat there resting, with aching feet and a pounding head. I looked at the sacred books and felt estranged from them; I seemed to have forgotten my studies.

Suddenly I realized that I had done something

wrong, and felt contemptuous of myself. I made a resolution then to which I still adhere: never do anything for money that goes against the grain, and avoid favors and presents. I wanted to relieve myself as soon as possible of the miserable job.

When I arrived home, Mother happened to be out and Father, in his study, looked at me anxiously, asking, "Where were you all day?" Then he blurted, "I'm sorry about the whole thing. You've got to continue studying . . ."

Emptying my pockets, I discovered that I had collected more in a day than the collector had given us in a month. Without counting the money, Father shoved it into a drawer. I felt relieved.

"I can't do it any more," I said.

"God forbid!"

But the new collector also stole. Finally Father put up a notice that no more money should be given the collector. He tried to get along on his fees from lawsuits, weddings, and divorces, but our situation grew worse, and even though he took pupils they did not remain with him very long. Mother went on a trip to Bilgoray to get help from her father and stayed there for weeks.

At home there was chaos. We lived on dry food and there was no one to supervise me. My sister, Hinde Esther, had married the son of a Warsaw Hasid and they were living in Antwerp, Belgium. I suddenly felt a great urge to study. I began in some inexplicable way to "read" a page from the Talmud by myself and even to understand a commentary explaining it. I examined Maimonides's *The Strong Hand* and other books I had not understood until then. One day in my father's bookcase I found a volume of the Cabala, *The Pillar of Service* by Reb Baruch Kosower. Although I missed the meaning of most of it, I did understand a little. A part of my brain that had been sealed seemed to be opening. I now experienced the profound joy of learning . . .

The Strong Ones

At cheder

CHEDER, too often described as a place where innocent children suffered at the hands of a sloppy, ill-tempered teacher, was not quite that. What was wrong with society was wrong with cheder.

There was one boy with constantly clenched fists who kept looking for a chance to hit someone. Assistant bullies and sycophants surrounded him.

Another boy, for whom it was not practical to use violence, acted the little saint, smiling at everyone, doing favors, and all with an expression that implied immeasurable love. But in his quiet way he schemed to acquire things, to taste something wonderful for nothing. Pious though he was, he showed friendship for the bully while feigning sympathy for his victims. When his friend the bully decided to give someone a bloody nose, the little saint would run to the victim with a handkerchief while gently admonishing the bully, "You shouldn't have done that . . ."

There was another boy who was interested only in business, trading a button for a nail, a bit of putty for a pencil, a candy for a roll. He was always losing out on bargains, but in the end he got the best of everyone. Half the cheder was indebted to him, since he lent money on interest. He and the bully had an arrangement whereby anyone who reneged had his hat snatched off.

Then there was the liar who boasted that his family was rich and famous and that Warsaw's elite visited his home. Promising us dates, figs, St. John's bread, and oranges from theoretical weddings and circumcisions, and a projected summer vacation, he demanded advance presents from all of us.

Then there was the victim. One day the bully drew blood from him and the next day he gave the bully a present. Smiling with sly submissiveness, the victim indicated another boy who needed a beating.

From my seat in cheder I saw everything, and even though the bully had punched me, I presented him with neither smiles nor gifts. I called him an Esau and predicted that his hereafter would be spent on a bed of nails. He hit me again for that, but I didn't weaken. I would have nothing to do with the bully, the priggish saint, the moneylender, or the liar, nor would I pay them any compliments.

I wasn't making out too well. Most of the cheder boys had grown hostile, informing against me to the teacher and the tutor. If they caught me in the street, they said, they'd break my leg. I recognized the danger. After all, I was too small to take on the entire cheder.

The trip to cheder each morning was agonizing, but I couldn't complain to my parents—they had their own troubles. Besides, they'd probably say, "That's what you get for being different from everyone else . . ."

There was nothing to do but wait it out. Even the devil had to weary. God, if He supported truth and justice, must inevitably side with me.

The day came when it seemed to me impossible to go on. Even the teacher, in that hellish atmosphere, opposed me, though I knew my Pentateuch. The rebbetzin made malicious remarks about me. It was as if I were excommunicated.

Then, one day, everything changed. The bully miscalculated the strength of a new boy, who just happened to hit back. Then the teacher hurled himself at the bully, who already had a lump on his head. He was dragged to the whipping bench, his pants were pulled down, and he was whipped before all of us. Like Haman, he was punished. When he tried to resume his reign of terror, he was repulsed in favor of the victor.

The moneylender also met his downfall. The father of one boy who had paid out too much interest appeared at cheder to complain. A search of the moneylender's pockets proved so fruitful that he too was whipped.

The saint's hypocrisy was recognized at last, despite his whispered secrets and his flatteries.

Then, as if in response to my prayers, the boys began speaking to me once more. The flatterers and the traders offered me good will and bargains—I don't know why. I might even have formed a group of my own, but I wasn't inclined that way. There was only one boy whose friendship I wanted, and he was the one I chose. Mendel was a fine, decent person without social ambitions. We studied from the same Pentateuch and walked with our arms about each other. Others, jealous, intrigued against us, but our friendship remained constant. We were like David and Jonathan . . .

Even after I left cheder, our friendship persisted. I had attended several cheders, and from each one I retained a friend. Occasionally, in the evenings, we would meet near the markets and walk along the sidewalk, talking, making plans. My friends' names were Mendel Besser, Mottel Horowitz, Abraham something-or-other, Boruch-Dovid, and others. More or less their leader, I would tell them things my older brother had told my mother. There was a great feeling of trust among us, until one day I had the impression that they resented me. They grumbled about my bossiness; I had to be demoted a little. They were preparing a revolution and I saw it in their faces. And even though I asked how I had offended them, they behaved like Joseph's brothers and could not answer in a friendly way. They couldn't even look at me directly. What was it they envied? My dreams . . . I could actually hear them say as I approached them, "Behold this dreamer cometh . . . Let us slay him and cast him in some pit . . . Let us sell him to the Ishmaelites . . ."

It is painful to be among one's brothers when they are jealous. They had been good to me, they praised me, and then they were mean. All at once they grew angry. Turning away as I approached, they whispered . . .

Friendships with me are not casual; I cannot make new friends easily. I wondered if I had sinned against them, or deceived them. But, if so, why hadn't they told me what was wrong?

I could not recollect having harmed them in any way, nor had I said anything against them. And if someone had slandered me, why should my friends believe it? After all, they were devoted to me.

There was nothing to do but wait it out. My kind has to become accustomed to loneliness. And when one is alone there is nothing to do but study. I became a diligent scholar. I would spend whole days in the Radzymin study house and then pore over religious works at home. Purchasing and renting books from peddlers, I read constantly. It was summertime and the days were long. Reading a story of three brothers, I imagined that I could write too, and began to cover both sides of a sheet. "Once there was a king who had three sons. One was wise, one foolish, and one merry . . ." But somehow the story didn't jell.

On another paper I began to draw freakish humans and fantastic beasts. But this too wearied me, and going out to the balcony, I looked down at the street. Only I was alone. Other boys were running, playing, and talking together. I'll go mad, I thought— there was too much happening in my head all the time. Shouldn't I jump from the balcony? Or spit down on the janitor's cap?

That evening, at the Radzymin study house, a

boy approached me, acting as a go-between. He spoke tactfully, suggesting that my friends were eager for an understanding but, since I was the minority, it was up to me to make the first move. In short, he suggested that I submit a plea for a truce.

I was infuriated. "It wasn't I who started this," I said. "Why should I be the one to make up?"

"You'll regret it," he warned.

"Leave!" I commanded.

He left angrily. His job as a trucemaker had been spoiled. But he knew I meant what I said.

Now that they had sent an intermediary, I knew my friends were remorseful. But I would never give in to them.

I grew accustomed to being alone and the days no longer seemed interminable. I studied, wrote, read stories. My brother had brought home a two-volume book called *Crime and Punishment*. Although I didn't really understand it, it fascinated me. Secluded in the bedroom, I read for hours. A student who had killed a crone suffered, starved, and reasoned profoundly. Coming before the prosecutor, he was questioned . . . It was something like a storybook, but different. Strange and lofty, it reminded me of the Cabala. Who were the authors of books like this, and who could understand them? Now and then a passage was illuminated for me, I understood an episode and became enthralled by the beauty of a new insight.

I was in another world. I forgot about my friends.

At evening services in the Radzymin study house, I was unaware of the men among whom I stood. My mind was wandering, when suddenly the intermediary approached.

"Nothing you have to say can interest me," I said.

"Here's a note," he told me.

It was like a scene from a novel. My friends wrote that they missed me. "We wander about in a daze . . ." I still remember what they said. Despite this great triumph, I was so immersed in my book that it scarcely seemed important any more that they wanted to make amends. I went out to the courtyard, and there they were. It reminded me of Joseph and his brothers. They had come to Joseph to buy grain, but why had my friends come to me?

Nevertheless, they did come, ashamed and somehow afraid—Simon, Levi, Judah. . . . Since I had not become Egypt's ruler, they were not required to bow down to the earth. I had nothing to sell but new dreams.

We talked together late and I spoke of my book. "This is no storybook, this is literature . . ." I said. I created for them a fantastic mélange of incidents and my own thoughts, and infected them with my excitement. Hours passed. They begged me to forgive them, confessed that they had been wrong and never would be angry with me again . . .

They kept their word.

Only time separated us. The rest was accomplished by the German murderers.

Reb Itchele and Shprintza

A Talmudic scholar

ow did a pious Jew get hot tea on the Sabbath, when cooking is forbidden? In small towns a basin of hot water was placed in the oven, along with the Sabbath meal, and in the city, teahouses kept hot water on the stove in a big kettle. The stoves were heated on Friday before sundown, so the water stayed hot all through the Sabbath.

As the young men and girls drank tea in the teahouses, they smiled at each other and conversed. Children would be arriving with teapots to buy hot water on credit, since it is forbidden to carry money on the Sabbath.

After the Sabbath midday meal, my father always sent me to buy our hot water at Itchele's grocery store. Itchele's combination store, home, and teahouse was located at 15 Krochmalna Street. His wife, Shprintza, a large, harassed, untidy woman who was in a constant state of excitement, was known for her good heart. Through hard work, this woman was able to support a large family. One of her sons, Noah, had gone to cheder with me.

Shprintza did everything: carried babies, bore

them, worked in the grocery, stocked the store, pickled cucumbers, made sauerkraut, minded the Sabbath kettle, and even found time for charity.

She was always preoccupied. With one eye she would watch a customer who was sloshing her hand about in the brine, trying to pick out a herring from the bottom of the barrel, and with the other eye, boys who liked to play with the beans in the sacks.

Shprintza was forever being forced to chastise fussy customers who behaved as if the goods in her store belonged to them. She waddled about in a decrepit, stained apron and a pair of battered shoes. Her hands were as large and tough as a man's. Her matron's wig was always disheveled.

A foreign traveler, coming upon a store with such a proprietress, surely would have thought her a barbarian, but Shprintza was a civilized and virtuous woman. Her life was dedicated to the highest of all tasks, that of supporting her family and—to the extent she could—Jewishness and the study of the Torah.

Her husband, Reb Itchele, was supposedly a merchant, but his days were spent in praying, arranging banquets for Hasidim, discussing saints, and studying the Mishnah. He was as small as his wife was large. He was as busy with Hasidic affairs as she was with storekeeping. A man who aspired to do everything at once, Itchele recited the Zohar, listened to the stories of Reb Meir the Eunuch, and pondered the interpretation of a difficult verse while collecting a few gulden for some pauper.

Shprintza never got away from her pickle barrels, sacks of provisions, bundles of wood, and customers. Reb Itchele, red-haired in youth, already had a yellow-gray beard when I knew him. He walked with short, quick strides. When he prayed at the study house, he swallowed many of his words; others he kept repeating as he paced back and forth, clapping his hands and raising his ritual fringes swiftly to his brow. His keen ear detected when it was his turn to answer amen. In God's house, as well as in the grocery, he kept his eye on everything, so that he would not fail to take part in some pious act.

During the week this couple was so busy it was impossible to speak to either the man or the wife. But when I came with my teapot on the Sabbath, things were very different.

The family lived in a small apartment in back of the store. If I remember correctly, they had only a single room, where the stove stood with the kettle on it. But a mood of Sabbath repose hovered over this room and its covered table, its benediction cup, and its bread knife with a mother-of-pearl handle.

Shprintza would be wearing a neatly combed wig and a Sabbath dress decorated with arabesques. Reb Itchele would have on a satin capote and a fur-edged hat.

The couple had two daughters, pious girls, almost the same age. When I was still a very small boy, these girls would ask me the same question every Sabbath. "Which of us would you prefer as a bride?"

Embarrassed, I would point to the smaller of the two.

"Why her?" the taller would ask, and I would reply, "You're too big."

My answer always evoked laughter.

But as I grew older, the question was asked less frequently, until finally I was considered too old for such jokes. Nevertheless, the girls and I never forgot the little game we had played and we would feel both constrained and roguish whenever we were in one another's company.

In this household, as in mine, Jewishness and worldliness were forever at odds.

Reb Itchele's oldest son refused to study the Talmud, became an artisan, and shaved off his beard. On Friday evenings, after the Sabbath candles had been lit, I would see this young man sitting in the shop of Zeitag the barber, being lathered and shaved. He caused Reb Itchele and Shprintza unutterable grief.

Sabbath afternoons he sat at their table, wearing a modern cap on his pomaded hair, a modern jacket, a paper collar, and a paper dickey. He was in a rush to get done both with the meal and with the table chants so he could take his young lady to that new sensation, the moving pictures. Reb Itchele avoided looking at this young rebel but dared not drive him from the house, fearful that what he would do next would land his parents in Gehenna.

Nor did Itchele and Shprintza derive much satisfaction from their younger son, Noah, my former classmate in cheder. True, Noah was still only a boy, but he did not want to study either, and they had been forced to take him out of school. He also refused to wear sidelocks.

I remember one Sabbath afternoon in particular. Entering Reb Itchele's back room, I said, "Good Sabbath. May I have some hot water?"

"Why do you have to tell us you want hot water?" Reb Itchele chanted. "Don't you think we know already?"

Shprintza rushed to my defense. "What do you want him to say?"

"Good Sabbath is enough."

"All right, then, good Sabbath."

"Good Sabbath, good year," replied Reb Itchele. "It is written that when the Messiah comes, all the days of the week will be one continual Sabbath."

"When will the people cook?" one of the daughters inquired.

"Who'll want to cook? This world will be a paradise. The saints, seated at God's table, will partake of Leviathan as they listen to the angels divulge the secrets of the Torah."

"Eva, draw him some water," Shprintza commanded.

"What's the hurry?" Reb Itchele asked. "How is your father, eh?"

"So-so."

"A wonderful man. A sage. Do you intend to follow in his footsteps?"

"Yes."

"What are you doing after dinner?"

"Nothing."

"Why don't you and Noah study together? To study by oneself is good, but if one does it with another, it is even nobler."

"Not today, Papa," Noah said.

"Why not?"

"I have to visit a friend."

"Who is he? Where are you supposed to meet? It is written that because God wanted to bestow his grace upon the Jews, he gave them the Torah and the Commandments. Why don't you accept His gift? If someone offered you a sackful of pearls and gold coins, would you tell him to keep them until you got back from visiting some boy? Gold and diamonds have value only in this world. When one dies, one takes nothing with him. But the Torah and the Commandments follow a person beyond the grave."

"Yes, Papa, but he expects me."

"What does he want? Who is he? What do you do together?"

I knew very well what Noah did. He had a pocketful of buttons decorated with crowns and eagles and he played with these buttons the entire Sabbath through. He also hung around the fellows who took girls to moving pictures.

He boasted that he had hitched rides on the back of droshkies on the Sabbath. What transgressions hadn't Noah committed? And here sat Reb Itchele staring disapprovingly at him from under his yellow brows.

"Nu, what did you say?"

"Another time."

"Well, if you don't want to, so be it. Eva, give the boy his hot water."

Eva took my teapot and filled it.

"Tell your father that next Tuesday is the anniversary of our rabbi's death and, God willing, there'll be a memorial banquet," Reb Itchele said.

"I'll tell him."

"Do you still go to cheder?"

"No, I'm reading the Talmud by myself."

"Do you hear that, Noah? Which part of the Talmud are you studying?"

"The part that concerns an egg laid on a holiday."

"Do you understand what you're reading?"

"Yes, I understand. If I'm confused about something, I look it up in Rashi's commentary."

"And if you don't understand Rashi's commentary?"

"I ask my father."

"Of course. 'Ask thy father and he shall tell thee.' But a generation has grown up that refuses to ask the father. Nowadays the father knows nothing, only the loafers are smart. What becomes of a Jew when he abandons his religion? To the Gentiles he remains a stranger. He has neither this world nor the world to come. Well, hurry along—your water is getting cold."

"Regards to your mother," Shprintza called after me.

Through the half-draped door I could see into the

store, where all week long customers swarmed under the gas lights, but which now was filled with Sabbath shadows and an eerie stillness. All the objects there appeared to have withdrawn into a Sabbathlike contemplation, particularly those it was forbidden to touch on this holy day. Everything emanated peace, the packages of chicory and yeast, the sacks of peas, the piles of kindling. God rested on the seventh day and so did they . . . Would a time really come when there would be only one eternal Sabbath?

Outside I saw Reb Meir the Eunuch. This man was a great enigma to me, a man who grew no beard. What could be odder than a beardless Jew? Moreover, he was out of his mind for two weeks out of every month. When deranged, he would mumble to himself, smile, and rub his hands. When he was in possession of himself, he poured forth wisdom, quotations from the Torah, Hasidic witticisms, tales of Wonder Rabbis.

Today was apparently one of his sane days. He passed wearing a satin capote and a fur-trimmed cap. It was his custom to pray at the study house until late in the afternoon. Only then did he return home.

But where was home? Who did he go to? He had no wife and certainly no children. Who prepared the Sabbath meal for him? Who would take in a eunuch, and a crazy one besides? Someone was willing to have him, watch over him, do his laundry, make his bed at night. Somewhere some merciful woman had assumed this task.

"Good Sabbath, Reb Meir."

"Good Sabbath. You've finished eating already?

Remind your father that next week is the anniversary of the rabbi's death, and there'll be a banquet."

And Reb Meir the Eunuch headed home to recite the benediction over the wine and to sing the Sabbath hymns. Eunuch or not, sane or insane, a Jew is a Jew.

The Mysteries of the Cabala

Coal porters

VERYONE knew us on Krochmalna Street. My friend Mendel and I walked there every day for hours, my hand on his shoulder, his on mine. We were so preoccupied telling each other stories that we stumbled into baskets of fruits and vegetables belonging to the market women, who shouted after us, "Are you blind or something, you slobs?"

I was ten or so. Mendel was already eleven. I was lean, white-skinned, with a scrawny neck, blue eyes, fiery red hair. My sidelocks were always flying as if in a wind; my gaberdine went unbuttoned, its pockets loaded with storybooks I rented two for a penny. Not only could I read a page of the Talmud by myself, I kept on trying my father's volumes of the Cabala, still without understanding much. On the end pages of these books I would draw, with colored pencils, six-winged angels, animals with two heads and with eyes in their tails, demons with horns, snouts, snakes' bodies, calf's feet. In the evening, when I stood on our balcony, I stared up into the star-studded sky and brooded about what there was before the creation of the world. At home everybody said I was growing up

125

to be a crazy philosopher, like that professor in Germany who pondered and philosophized for years, until he arrived at the conclusion that a man should walk with his head down and his feet up.

My friend Mendel was the son of a coal porter. Every few weeks his father brought a huge basket of coal for our stoves, and my mother gave him a kopeck. Mendel was taller than I, dark like a gypsy, his hair so black it had a bluish tinge. He had a short nose, a chin with a split in the middle, and slanting eyes like a Tartar's. He wore a tattered gaberdine and torn boots. His family lived in one room at 13 Krochmalna Street. His mother, blind in one eye, dealt in crockery in a stall behind the markets.

We both had the same passion: inventing stories. We never got tired of listening to each other's tales. That late afternoon in summer, as we passed Yanash's bazaar, Mendel halted. He had a secret to tell me: It was not true his father was a coal porter. That was only a disguise. Actually he was richer than any Rothschild. His family had a palace in the forest, and another castle on the sea, full of gold, silver, and diamonds. I asked Mendel how they had become so rich, and he said, "Swear by your fringed garment you will never tell anyone."

I swore.

"Let's split a straw."

We picked up a straw and, each taking an end, tore it between us as a bond. In Mendel's Tartar eyes a

dreamy smile appeared and he opened a mouth of extremely white teeth, just like a gypsy's. He said, "My father is a robber."

A shiver ran down my back. "Who does he rob?"

"He digs tunnels into banks and drags out their gold. He hides in the forest, waiting to ambush merchants. He wears a gun and a sword. He is a sorcerer, too, and he can enter the trunks of trees, even though no one can see any opening."

"So why does he have to be a porter?" I asked.

"So the police won't find out . . ."

Mendel told me that his father did not operate singlehanded. He was the chief of twelve hundred thieves, whom he sent all over the world to rob people and bring back the booty. Some sailed the seas and attacked ships; others held up caravans in the desert. Mendel said that, besides his mother, his father had twelve concubines, captive princesses. And when he, Mendel, became Bar Mitzvah, he would also become a robber. He would marry a princess from the other side of the River Sambation. She was already waiting for Mendel to come to the palace and wed her. She had golden hair falling to her ankles and wore golden slippers on her feet. To keep her from running away, Mendel's father had bound her to a pillar with a chain.

"Why does she want to run away?" I asked.

"Because she is yearning for her mother."

I knew it was all lies and even realized which storybooks the different parts came from, but his story enchanted me all the same. We were standing near the fish market, where carp, pike, and chub swam in tubs 127

of water. It was Thursday and women were buying fish for the Sabbath. A blind beggar wearing dark glasses, with a cottony gray beard, plucked chords on a mandolin as he sang a heartrending song about the sinking of the *Titanic*. On his shoulder stood a parrot picking at its feathers with its beak. The beggar's wife, young and as agile as a dancer, collected alms in a tambourine. Over the Wola section, the sun was setting, larger than usual, as yellow as gold. Farther out lay a huge, sulphur-yellow cloud blazing like a fiery river upon a bed of glowing coals. It made me think of the River of Fire in Gehenna, where the wicked are punished.

Mendel and I, even though we were best friends, were also silently engaged in a struggle. He was envious of me because my father was a rabbi and because we lived in an apartment with two rooms, a kitchen, and a balcony. He was always trying to prove that he was the stronger, cleverer, and more learned one. Now I was trying to invent a story as wonderful as Mendel's, or even more so. Abruptly I said, "I also have a secret I've never told you."

Mendel's Tartar eyes filled with mockery. "What's your secret?"

"Swear you won't tell anyone."

Mendel swore with a false smile and a look that almost seemed to be winking at someone unseen.

I said: "I know the Cabala!"

Mendel's eyes narrowed into slits. "You? How could you know it?"

"My father taught it to me."

"Is it allowed—to teach a boy the Cabala?"

"I'm different from other boys."

"Well . . . ! So what did you learn?"

"I can create pigeons. I can make wine flow from the wall. I can recite a spell and fly up in the air."

"What else?"

"I can take seven-mile steps."

"What else?"

"I can turn invisible. And I can change pebbles into pearls."

Mendel began to twist one of his sidelocks. Just as mine were disheveled, his were twirled tightly like two little horns.

"If that's so, you could have more money than the richest man in the world."

"Yes. True."

"So why haven't you got it?"

"One is not allowed to make use of the Cabala. It's very dangerous. There is one spell that if you utter it the sky turns red like fire, the sea begins to churn, and the waves rise until they touch the clouds. All the animals drown; all the buildings collapse; an abyss opens and the whole world becomes black as midnight."

"How does that spell go?"

"Do you want me to destroy the world?"

"Nnnn . . . no."

"When I'm older, I will get permission from the prophet Elijah to fly to the Holy Land. There I will live in a ruin and bring the Messiah."

Mendel bent his head. He picked up a piece of paper from the sidewalk and began to fold it into a bird. I expected him to ask many more questions, but he remained stubbornly silent. All at once I felt that in my ambition I had overdone it; it was Mendel's fault. He had driven me to try to make myself too great. My own words had frightened me. One is not allowed to play games with the Cabala. Terrible nightmares might invade my sleep. I said, "Mendel, I want to go home."

"Let's go."

We moved toward the gate that led to Mirowski Street, no longer walking with our arms about each other's shoulders, but a little apart. Instead of drawing us closer, our talk had separated us. But why? I suddenly noticed how ragged Mendel's clothes were. The toe of his left boot had opened like a mouth and the nails stuck up like teeth. We came out on Mirowski Street, which was littered with horse dung, straw off farmers' carts, rotten fruit thrown out by the fruit merchants. Between the two city markets stood a building where ice was manufactured. Though it was still day outside, inside the electric lights were burning. Wheels turned rapidly; leather conveyor belts flowed; signals lit up and extinguished themselves. Not a single person was to be seen. Uncanny noises came from in there. Under our feet, through grates, we could see into cellars where tanks full of water were turning to ice. For quite a while Mendel and I stood there gawking; then we moved on. I asked suddenly, "Who feeds her?"

Mendel seemed to wake up. "What are you talking about?"

"I mean the girl with the golden slippers."

"There are maidservants there."

Not far from the second market, I saw two coins, two copper six-groschen pieces that lay side by side as if someone had placed them on the sidewalk. I bent down and picked them up. Mendel, seeing them too, cried out, "Partners!"

I gave him one immediately, though at the same time I thought that if it had been he who had picked them up, he would not have given me one. Mendel looked at the coin from every angle and then he said, "If you can turn pebbles into pearls, what do you want a six-groschen for?"

I would have liked to ask him: And if your father is such a rich robber, what do *you* want a six-groschen for? But something held me back. I was suddenly aware how yellowish his skin was and what high cheekbones he had. Something in that face spoke to me, but what it was saying I couldn't grasp. The lobes of his ears were attached to his cheeks; the wings of his nostrils rose and fell like a horse's. The corners of his mouth curled with envy and his black eyes scorned me. He asked, "What are you going to buy with your money? Candy?"

"I will give it to charity," I answered.

"Here—here's a poor man."

In the middle of the sidewalk, on a board with little wheels, sat half a man; he looked as if he had been sawed across the middle. Both hands gripped pieces of wood padded with cloth, on which he leaned. He wore his cap visor over his eyes, and a torn jacket. On his neck hung a cup to throw alms in. I knew very well what could be bought for six groschen—colored pencils, storybooks, halvah—but some pride ordered me not to hesitate. Stretching my arm out, I tossed the coin in the cup. The cripple, as if afraid I might change my mind and ask for it back, rolled away so quickly that he almost knocked somebody over.

Mendel's eyebrows came together. "When do you study the Cabala? At night?"

"After midnight."

"So what's going on in heaven?"

I lifted my eyes to the sky and it was red, with black and blue streaks across the middle, as if a storm were coming. Two birds flapped up, screeching, calling each other. The moon had come out. Only a minute ago it had been day. Now night had fallen. The women at the street stands were cleaning up their merchandise. A man with a long stick was walking from one lamppost to the next, lighting the gas flames. I wanted to answer Mendel but couldn't think what to say. I was ashamed of my pretending, as though I were suddenly a grown-up. I said, "Mendel, enough of these lies."

"What's the matter, huh?"

"I don't study the Cabala and your father is not a robber."

Mendel stopped. "Why are you so angry? Because you gave your six-groschen to the beggar?"

132   "I'm not angry. If you have a palace in the forest,

you don't carry coals all day long for Haim Leib. And you haven't got a girl with golden slippers. It's all a fairy story."

"So you want to quarrel? Don't think just because your father is a rabbi I'm going to flatter you. Maybe I have lied, but you'll never know the truth."

"What is there to know? You made it all up."

"I'll become a bandit, a real one."

"They will roast you in Gehenna."

"Let them roast me. I'm in love!"

I looked at him, shocked. "You're lying again."

"No, it's the truth. If not, may God strike me dead on the spot."

I knew Mendel would not swear such an oath in vain. I felt cold, as if someone with icy fingers had touched my ribs. "With a girl?"

"What else? With a boy? She lives in our court-yard. We'll get engaged. We'll go to my brother's in America."

"Aren't you ashamed . . . ?"

"Jacob also was in love. He kissed Rachel. It is written in the Bible."

"Girl-chaser!"

And I began to run. Mendel screamed something after me and I even imagined that he was pursuing me. I ran until I reached the Radzymin study house. Near the door Mendel's father was praying, a tall, lean man with a sharp Adam's apple, a bent back, and a face that was coal black, like a chimney sweep's. His loins were girded with a rope. He shook, leaned

133

forward, and beat his chest. I imagined he must be asking God's forgiveness for the blasphemies of his son.

At the east wall stood my father in a velvet gaberdine, wearing a broad-brimmed hat and a white sash about his waist. His head touched the wall as he swayed back and forth. A single candle burned in the menorah. No, I did not yet know the Cabala. But I knew that everything that was happening to me tonight was filled with its mysteries. I felt a deep sadness such as I had never felt before. When my father finished praying, I walked over to him and said, "Papa, I have to talk to you."

At my serious tone, my father looked at me out of his blue eyes. "What's the matter?"

"Papa, I want you to teach me the Cabala."

"So that's it? At your age it is forbidden to study the Cabala. It is written that these mysteries should not be divulged to a man before he is thirty."

"Papa, I want it now."

My father clutched his red beard. "What's your hurry? You can be a decent man without the Cabala."

"Papa, can one destroy the world with a holy spell?"

"The ancient saints could do everything. We can do nothing. Come, let's go home."

We moved toward the gate, where Rebecca, the baker's daughter, stood with baskets full of fresh rolls, bread, bagels warm from the oven. Women were picking over the baked goods and their crusts crackled. My father and I walked out into the street, where the gas lamps cast a yellow glow. Between two chimneys spouting smoke and sparks hung a large, blood-red moon.

"Is it true that people live there?" I asked.

My father was silent for a while. "What makes you think so? Nothing is known. Cabala is only for strong brains. When weak little brains are immersed in the Cabala—one can easily fall into insanity."

My father's words frightened me. I felt myself close to madness.

He said, "You are still a boy. When, God willing, you grow up, get married, have more sense, then you will find out what you can do."

"I'm not going to get married."

"What else? Stay a bachelor? It is written: 'He created it not in vain. He formed it to be inhabited.' You will grow up, be matched with a girl, and get engaged."

"What girl?"

"Who can know in advance?"

At that moment I realized why I was so sad. The street was full of girls but I didn't know who was going to be my betrothed. She, the one destined for me, didn't know either. It could be that we both bought candy in the same store, that we passed each other, looked at each other, not knowing that we were going to be man and wife. I began to look among the crowd. The street was full of girls my age, some a little younger, some older. One walked and licked an ice-cream cone. Another one nibbled cheese cake at Esther's candy store, holding it between her thumb

135

and middle finger, with her pinky lifted up elegantly. A girl carrying books and notebooks under her arm, with red ribbons in her braids, a pleated skirt and a black apron, had black-stockinged legs that looked like a doll's. The streets were full of the aroma of fresh bagels, of breezes coming from the Vistula and the Praga forest. Around the street lamps a myriad of winged creatures—moths, butterflies, gnats—whirled, deceived by the light into believing night was day. I looked at the upper floors, where girls stood on balconies, gazed out of windows. They were talking, singing, laughing. I listened to the noise of sewing machines, to a gramophone playing. Behind a window I saw the dark shadow of a girl. I imagined she was staring at me through the mesh of the curtain. I said to my father, "Papa, can you find out from the Cabala who you are going to get engaged to?"

My father stopped. "What do you have to know for? They know in heaven and that is enough."

For a while we walked in silence. Then my father asked, "Son, what has happened to you?"

All the lampposts became bent and all the lights foggy as my eyes filled with tears. "Papa, I don't know."

"You are growing up, my son. That is what is happening to you."

And my father suddenly did something he had never done before: he bent down and kissed my forehead.

The Satin Coat

Chanting in the synagogue

I T was our clothes that made our poverty apparent. Food was cheap, nor were we big eaters. Mother prepared a soup with potatoes, browned flour, and fried onions. Only on Passover did we eat eggs. True, a pound of meat cost twenty kopecks, but it produced a lot of broth. Flour, buckwheat, chickpeas, beans were not expensive.

But clothes were dear.

My mother would wear a dress for years and take such good care of it that it still looked new. A pair of shoes lasted her three years. Father's satin capote was somewhat frayed, but so were the capotes and skullcaps of most of the congregation at the nearby Radzymin study house. It was worse for us children. My boots wore out every three months. Mother complained that other children were careful but I messed up everything.

At the Radzymin study house, on the Sabbath, boys wore satin or silk gaberdines, velvet hats, polished boots, and sashes. I went in a gaberdine that was too small for me. Now and again I did get a new piece of clothing, but not until what I had was nothing but rags.

141

But there was one time just before Passover when suddenly we got lucky.

This was always a good period of the year for us, for Father would get commissions for selling to a Gentile—our janitor, to be exact—people's hametz; that is, all those items, such as unleavened bread, flour, kneading boards, and rolling pins, that are not permitted in a Jewish household during Passover. There was a certain element of the spurious in this transaction because immediately after Passover all this property reverted to its original owners.

From listening to those who came to sell their hametz, I learned how little we had, in comparison to them. They had to dispose of whisky, cherry brandy, preserves; we, nothing but a few pots and pans. Occasionally someone listed a stable with horses, although I am uncertain how a horse can possibly be considered a hametz. But, it's true, horses do eat oats. There was one man whose son was traveling with a circus and who felt it necessary to declare as hametz the entire menagerie.

Why was this particular Passover a lucky one for us? To begin with, we had received many fine gifts on Purim, which precedes Passover by only four weeks. But best of all, Jonathan, a tailor from Leoncin, where my father had once been rabbi, had moved to Warsaw. Jonathan, a tall, slender man with a pock-marked face, a spare beard, and brilliant eyes, dressed like a Hasid, not like a tailor. On the Sabbath he wore a satin capote; he took snuff, went to visit the Radzymin rabbi on holidays, and was, in fact, a learned man. Now that he was in Warsaw, he visited my father to discuss erudite matters. Seeing the condition of my wardrobe, Jonathan offered to clothe me on credit. We could pay for the material at our convenience.

What a stroke of luck! As he measured me, he beamed proudly, treating me as though I were a member of his own family. He had, as a matter of fact, been present at my circumcision. Noting my various measurements in chalk, he remarked to my mother, "Oh Rebbetzin, how the years do fly."

Jonathan apparently had no other work at the moment, for almost immediately after taking my measurements he had me down to his house for a fitting, testing me on my Hebrew at the same time, appreciative of the opportunity to use a few Hebrew phrases of his own and discourse in a scholarly way. Although he was only a tailor, he had a great love for Judaism and savored every Hebrew word. At the time of his marriage he had been familiar with only the required prayers, but later he studied the Scriptures in Yiddish, learned the Mishnah with a teacher, and got help from students. Ridiculed in Leoncin for his aspirations, he proved despite this that it is never too late to learn. Father had been one of those who helped Jonathan transform himself into a scholar, and the tailor was eager to show his gratitude.

His house was alive with girls, noise, and the odors of cooking. His three daughters, who had known me since early childhood and now saw me being outfitted like a man for a satin capote, could not keep from making comments. With their mother, they argued about whether the capote was the right length. My mother, in a lavish gesture, had also ordered new boots for me from Michael the cobbler. I was to look completely done over when I entered the study house on Passover.

Although I had had no great passion for clothes, I soon acquired one, becoming more intrigued with each new addition to my wardrobe. New shirts were being sewn for me by a seamstress, and my new velvet hat already lay in a box in the closet. I had visions of entering the study house triumphantly on Passover night, and amazing all the boys there. Previously, my clothes had made me feel inferior to them, even though I was more informed than they, knew about Zionism, socialism, the weight of air, and the origin of coal—having learned it all from my brother Joshua and an almanac. But now they would see that I could also have a new outfit for the holiday. Most tailors did not keep their word about having things ready for a holiday, but Jonathan was different.

All the same, I felt a premonition of disaster, for how could things go as smoothly as I dreamed them? But, on the other hand, what could go wrong, and why was I so apprehensive? Yes, of course, Jonathan might burn the cloth while pressing it, or the capote could even be stolen. From *The Rod of Punishment*, as well as from my own experience, I knew that the material world was full of snares. I had become too enamored of its pleasures.

Even so, things kept going smoothly. True to his

promise, Michael the cobbler delivered a pair of boots that gleamed as though lacquered. The satin capote already hung in our closet. Shortly before Passover, people began coming to our house to sell their hametz, and standing behind Father's chair, I watched the ceremony, which wasn't terribly complicated. The person selling the articles was told to touch the tip of a handkerchief, signifying that he agreed to sell his things to a Gentile. The bill of sale was begun, as follows: "The hametz of Reb so-and-so . . ." and in a mixture of Yiddish and Hebrew all the items were listed. I was sure I could do the job myself, if I had the chance.

The men would chat, sign, and talk about other Passovers. My father asked a deaf man if he had any alcohol to declare.

"Yes. A little wheat flour."

The others shouted into his ear, "Alcohol! Brandy!"

"Oh. Why didn't you say so? Of course I have alcohol."

A widow who came to sell her hametz didn't know how to sign her name, and Father told her to touch the pen, but she couldn't understand what he meant. Father repeated, "Just the shank of the pen, for a second."

She didn't know what "shank of the pen" meant. Efficient though she was in her stall at the market-place, she was bewildered by Father's study and all the men there. Mother came in and explained what had to be done, and the woman was greatly relieved, *145* and said, "Rebbetzin, I have no trouble understanding *you* . . ."

And she touched the pen.

Then, unknotting a kerchief, she counted out several copper coins. "Have a good Passover," she said to Father.

"May you live to see the next," he replied.

Suddenly, over her wind- and sun-ravaged face, the tears gushed, and everyone grew silent. After she left, Father said, "Who knows who is best-loved by God? She may be a saint . . ."

Mother reentered the study looking flushed and grimy, as she had come from stoking the stove to remove all traces of hametz. In the bedroom, the ordinary matzoh was suspended in sheets from the ceiling. The two portions of matzoh baked with extra care, to be eaten only by the most devout, had been put aside for Father and Mother. Mother, a rabbi's daughter, was granted this privilege usually reserved for men.

Everything went according to ritual. The night preceding Passover, Father searched the house, in the traditional manner, for hametz to be burned the next day. One was allowed to eat hametz until nine the next morning—and after that until sundown, neither hametz nor matzoh. From mashed potatoes, eggs, and sugar, Mother then prepared for us children a pancake that was indescribably delicious.

At sunset Passover began. So far nothing had gone wrong. I washed, put on a new shirt, new trousers, the new boots, the new velvet hat, and the satin capote that glistened festively. I had become a boy from a wealthy family, and I walked downstairs with my father. Neighbors, opening their doors to look at me, spat to ward off the evil eye; and the girls who sat on thresholds grating the traditional bitter herb, horse-radish, smiled as I went by, while their eyes teared from the horseradish. Girls my own age, who had so short a time before shared toys and pebbles with me, looked on with approval. Now that we were growing up, they were too shy to speak to me, but their glances were reminiscent.

My father and I went to the Radzymin study house, climbed the stairs, and tried the door. It was locked, and a notice hung there: "Gas out of order. Closed until after the holiday."

Closed on Passover night? The Radzymin study house? Incredible! We didn't know what to do, and remained there, confounded. *The Rod of Punishment* had been right. One should not depend on the comforts of the material world; there was nothing in it but dis-appointments. Only service to God mattered, and the study of the Torah. Everything else crumbled . . .

At the Minsk study house, where we went to pray, no one knew me or cared about my new outfit. There were a few boys I recognized, but, as strangers here, we all huddled near the exit.

It was a harsh blow and a lesson not to get involved in worldly vanities.

A Boy Philosopher

Israel Joshua Singer, in his twenties

Y brother Israel Joshua, because of his emancipated views, found it difficult to speak to my father, whose only response was, "Unbeliever! Enemy of Judaism!" On the other hand, my brother would have long talks with my mother, and often, in my presence, they would discuss me.

"What's to become of him?" my brother would argue. "Must he marry and open a store or become a teacher in a cheder? There are too many stores already and too many teachers. If you glance out the window, Mother, you can see what Jews look like—stooped, despondent, living in filth. Watch them drag their feet as they walk . . . Listen to them speak. It's no wonder everyone else thinks of them as Asiatics. And how long do you think Europe will stand for this clump of Asia in its midst?"

"Gentiles have always hated Jews," Mother said. "Even if a Jew wore a top hat, he'd be hated, because he stands for truth."

"What truth? Does anyone know what the truth is? Every religion has its own prophets and holy books.   *153*

Have you heard of Buddhism? Buddha was just like Moses and he performed miracles too."

Mother made a face as if she had some bad-tasting thing in her mouth. "How can you dare to compare them—an idol worshipper and the saint Moses? Woe is me! What my own flesh and blood says!"

"Listen, Mother. Buddha was no idol worshipper, he was a very profound thinker. He agreed with our own prophets. As for Confucius . . ."

"No more! Don't speak of those heathens in the same breath as our saints. The Buddha came from India . . . I remember that from *The Paths of the World*. They burn widows there and kill aged parents while everyone celebrates."

"You don't mean India."

"Who cares? They're all idolaters. A cow, to them, is a god. The Chinese, on the other hand, throw away their extra daughters. We Jews alone believe in one God; all the others worship trees, snakes, crocodiles, everything you can think of . . . They're all wicked. Even while they say, 'Turn the other cheek,' they murder each other and go on sinning. You want to compare them to us?"

"If we had our own country, we'd be involved in wars also. King David wasn't such a compassionate man . . ."

"Shush! Watch what you say! May God have mercy on you! Don't touch our anointed. King David and Solomon were both prophets. The Talmud says it is wrong to consider David a sinner . . ."

"I know what it says. But what about Bathsheba?"

Since that was my mother's name, every time I heard about Bathsheba I felt that Mother was somehow implicated. Mother's face flushed.

"Sh! You read idiotic books and repeat everything! King David will live forever and those trashy books aren't worth the paper they're printed on. Who are the authors? Loafers."

These discussions intrigued me. I had already discussed the subjects with my brother. I had no inclination to be a storekeeper or a Talmud teacher or have a "slovenly wife and a bunch of brats," as my brother put it. Once he said, "He'd better become a worker."

"With God's help he'll be a rabbi, not a worker. He takes after his grandfather," Mother said.

"A rabbi? Where? Everywhere there are rabbis. Why do we need so many?"

"And why so many workers? A rabbi, no matter how poor he is, is still better off than a shoemaker."

"Just wait until the workers unite."

"They'll never unite. Each one wants to steal the other's bread. Why don't soldiers unite and refuse to go to war?"

"Oh, that will come too."

"When? There's so much unnecessary killing. Every Monday and Thursday there's a Turkish crisis. The world is full of evil, that's all there is to it. We'll never find peace here—only in the other world."

"You're a pessimist, Mother."

"Wait, my soup is burning!"

How often I listened to discussions of this sort, with   155 each side effectively destroying the arguments of the other! But when it came to proving the case, what was relied on were easily disputed quotations. I remained silent, keeping my opinions to myself. The Gentiles were idol worshippers, true, but King David actually had sinned. And when Jews lived in their own country, they too had killed. And it was true that each religion had its own prophets, but who could say which ones had spoken to God? These were questions that Mother did not seem able to answer.

"What kind of trade appeals to you?" my brother asked. "How about becoming an engraver and carving letters on brass and copper?"

"Good."

"Or a watchmaker?"

"Too hard."

"You can learn it. How about a doctor?"

"Let him be. What do doctors know? They take money for nothing. Jews will always be Jews and they'll always need rabbis."

"In Germany, rabbis attend universities!" my brother announced proudly.

"I know those reform rabbis," my mother said. "They can find a way to permit eating meat with milk dishes, but how can they justify shaving, when it's contrary to Mosaic law? What kind of rabbi defies the Torah?"

"They use a kind of powder for shaving, not a razor."

"Are they ashamed of beards because they want to

look like Gentiles? If their rabbis are like that, I can imagine what the rest of them are like."

Suddenly Father appeared from his study. "Let's end these discussions once and for all," he cried out. "Tell me—who created the world? All they see is the body and they think that's all there is. The body is nothing but a tool. Without the soul, the body is like a slab of wood. The souls of those who gorge themselves and swill are evil and wander about in the desert, tortured by devils and hobgoblins. They've learned the truth too late. Even Gehenna is closed to them. The world is full of transmigrant souls . . ." Father said. "When a soul leaves a body unclean, it is returned to earth to wander about again, as a worm or a reptile, and its grief is tremendous . . ."

"Then, according to you, Father, God is wicked."

"Enemy of Israel! God loves man, but when man defiles himself, he must be cleansed."

"How can you expect a Chinaman to know the Torah?"

"Why worry about a Chinaman? Just think about God and His wonders. When I open a holy book I sometimes see a mite smaller than a pinpoint walking about. It too is a wonder of God. Can all the professors in the world get together and create one mite?"

"Well, what does it all add up to?"

After Father left and Mother went out to buy something, I asked my brother, "Who did create the mite?"

"Nature."

"And who created nature?"

"And who created God?" my brother rejoined. "Something had to come from itself, and later everything developed out of this original matter. From the energy of the sun, the first bacteria were created at the edge of the sea. Conditions happened to be favorable. Creatures fought among themselves and the strongest survived. Bacteria formed into colonies and a division of the functions began."

"But where did it all come from in the first place?"

"It was always like this; no one knows. Every people has made up its own rites. There was the rabbi, for example, who said you mustn't urinate in the snow on the Sabbath because it resembles plowing . . ."

Although later in my life I read a great deal of philosophy, I never found more compelling arguments than those that came up in my own kitchen. At home I even heard about strange facts that are in the province of psychic research. And after such discussions I would go outside to play; but as I went through the games of tag and hide-and-seek, my imagination was at work. What if I found the kind of water that made one wise and a party to all secrets, or if the prophet Elijah arrived to teach me all the Seven Wisdoms of the World? And what if I found a telescope that saw directly into heaven? My thoughts, which were not the thoughts of other boys, made me both proud and lonely. And always there were the ultimate questions: What is right? What must I do? Why does God remain silent in the Seventh Heaven? Once a man came up to me and asked, "What's the matter? Why do you think so hard? Are you afraid the sky will fall on you?"

The Shot at Sarajevo

Life in a Warsaw courtyard

OR a long time our family had discussed the possibility of moving from our apartment at 10 Krochmalna Street, where we used kerosene lamps because there was no gas and shared an outhouse in the courtyard with everyone else in the building. This outhouse was the bane of my childhood. It was dark there all the time, and filthy. Rats and mice were everywhere, overhead as well as on the floor. Many children, because of it, were stricken with constipation and developed nervous disorders.

The staircase was another plague, because certain children preferred it to the outhouse. To make things worse, there were women who used it as a garbage dump. The janitor, who was supposed to light lamps along the stairway, seldom did so, and when he did, we were deprived of them by 10:30. The tiny, smoke-stained lamps gave so little light that the darkness seemed to thicken around them. When I used this murky stairway, I was pursued by all the devils, evil spirits, demons, and imps of whom my parents spoke to prove that there is a God and life after death. Cats raced along beside me. From behind closed doors, one often heard a wailing for the dead. At the courtyard gate a funeral procession might be waiting. I was breathless by the time I reached my door. Nightmares began to come to me, so horrifying that I would wake from sleep drenched in sweat.

We found it hard enough to pay the twenty-four rubles a month rent for a front apartment and balcony; then how could we afford to move to 12 Krochmalna Street, a new building with gas lights and toilets, where the rent would be twenty-seven? However, we decided that changing our place would change our luck . . .

It was the spring of 1914.

The newspapers had for years referred to the explosive situation in the Balkans and the rivalry between England and Germany. But there were no newspapers in my home any more. It was my brother Israel Joshua who brought them there, and he had moved out after an argument with my father.

Everyone told us to change apartments. The No. 12 landlord, Leizer Przepiorko, was an Orthodox millionaire. Reputedly stingy, he had all the same never evicted a Jew. The superintendent, Reb Isaiah, was an old Kotzk Hasid, a friend of my father's. Since No. 12 had a gate that led to Mirowski Street, to the markets, Father would be rabbi for both Krochmalna and Mirowski Streets. Also, many lawsuits, weddings, and divorces were scheduled at that time, which meant extra money for us. We decided to move.

The new, ground-floor apartment, freshly painted,

faced a bakery, and the kitchen window looked out on a wall. There were five or six stories over us.

No. 12 was like a city. It had three enormous courtyards. The dark entrance always smelled of freshly baked bread, rolls, and bagels, caraway seed, and smoke. Koppel the baker's yeasty breads were always out in his courtyard, rising on boards. In No. 12 there were also two Hasidic study houses, the Radzymin and the Minsk, as well as a synagogue for those who opposed Hasidism. There was also a stall where cows were kept chained to the wall all year round. In some cellars, fruit had been stored by dealers from Mirowski Street; in others, eggs were preserved in lime. Wagons arrived there from the provinces. No. 12 swarmed with Torah, prayer, commerce, and toil. Kerosene lamps were unheard of. Some apartments even had telephones.

But it had not been an easy move, even though Nos. 10 and 12 adjoined. We had to load our things in a wagon, and some of them broke. Our wardrobe was unbelievably heavy, a fortress with lion heads on oaken doors and a cornice covered with engravings that weighed a ton. How it had been dragged from Radzymin is beyond me.

I will never forget lighting the two-jet gas lamp for the first time. I was dazzled and intimidated by the strange radiance that filled the apartment and even seemed to penetrate my skull. Demons would have a hard time hiding here.

The toilet delighted me. So did the gas oven in the

kitchen. It was not necessary any more to prepare kindling for tea or bring in coal. You only had to strike a match and watch the blue flame ignite. Nor would I have to drag jugs of kerosene from the store, since there was a gas meter where one inserted a forty-groschen piece to get gas. And I knew many people here because it was at the Radzymin study house in this courtyard that I had always prayed.

For a while, our predicted good luck came true. Father's lawsuits were numerous. Things went so well that year that he decided to enroll me in a cheder again. I was past cheder age, but at 22 Twarda Street there was a special cheder for older boys where the teacher lectured instead of studying with his pupils. Some of my friends from other cheders attended this one.

I was reading non-religious books at that time and had developed a taste for heresy; it was rather ridiculous, therefore, for me to be attending cheder again. My friends and I made fun of the teacher, who had a yellow beard and bulging eyes, spoke with a village accent, ate raw onions, and smoked stinking tobacco in a long pipe. He was divorced and matchmakers came to whisper secrets in his hairy ears . . .

Suddenly there were rumors of war. The Austrian Crown Prince had been shot, they said, in Serbia. Newspaper extras with huge headlines appeared, printed on only one side. In our discussions of politics, we boys decided that it would be preferable for Germany to win—what would be gained from Russian rule? German occupation would put all Jews into short jackets, and the *gymnasium* would be compulsory. What could be better than going to worldly schools in uniforms and decorated caps? At the same time we were convinced (much more than the German General Staff) that Germany's strength could never match the combined forces of Russia, France, and England. One boy speculated that because of their shared language it was only natural that America should step in to help England . . .

My father began to read newspapers. New words were prevalent—mobilization, ultimatum, neutrality. The rival governments sent notes. The kings wrote letters one to the other and called themselves Nicky and Willy. The common people—workers, porters— met in groups on Krochmalna Street to discuss conditions.

Suddenly it was the Ninth Day of Ab, the Sunday that is the postponed fast day. It was also the beginning of the First World War.

Women were everywhere, buying up food. Small though they were, they carried huge baskets of flour, groats, beans, and whatever else they could find in the stores, which were closed half the time. First the storekeepers rejected worn-out bank notes, then they demanded silver and gold instead of paper. They began hoarding their stock in order to increase prices.

People were in a festive mood, as if it were Purim. Weeping women trailed their husbands, bearded Jews with tiny white pins in their lapels, indicating that they had been called up for military service. Both annoyed and amused, these men strutted along while

169

behind them children carried sticks on their shoulders and called out military commands.

Running home from the Radzymin study house, my father announced that he had heard the war would be over in two weeks. "They have cannons that can kill a thousand Cossacks at one blow."

"Woe . . ." cried my mother. "What is the world coming to?"

Father consoled her: "Well, there won't be any more rent to pay, now that the government has made a moratorium . . ."

My mother went on, "And who will want lawsuits? Where will we get the money to eat?"

We were in trouble. There were no more letters from my sister, who had married and lived in Antwerp; and my twenty-one-year-old brother, Israel Joshua, was supposed to report to Tomaszow, my father's home town, for conscription in the Russian army. He decided to go into hiding instead. We had no money with which to stock up on food, as our neighbors were doing. Knowing how hungry I was going to become, I experienced an extraordinary gnawing appetite. I ate insatiably. Mother would come home flushed, moaning about the food shortage.

Now, for the first time, I began to hear unflattering bits of gossip about other Jews on the street. Jewish storekeepers, just like the Gentiles, were hiding goods, raising prices, trying to capitalize on the war. Moshe the paper dealer, who lived in our courtyard, boasted in the study house about his wife's purchase of five hundred rubles' worth of food. "Thank God," he said,

"I have provisions for a year. How much longer can the war last?" And he smilingly stroked his silver beard.

There was considerable confusion. Young men with blue cards were able to study the Talmud, but pale and concerned, the green-carded ones tried to lose weight to avoid the draft. Men who sold flour and groats were lucky, but not so the now unemployed bookbinders, teachers, and scribes. The Germans captured Kalisz, Będzin, and Częstochowa. I felt the burden of growing up and expected a mysterious catastrophe. It seemed to me that if only we had accepted the lack of toilets and gas in No. 10, we might have been spared all this . . .

This was the war between Gog and Magog, Father said. And every day he discovered new omens proving that the Messiah was soon to come . . .

Hunger

Studying at cheder

T turned out that the German occupation of Warsaw did not result in the Jews wearing modern dress and all Jewish boys being sent to *gymnasiums*. Jews remained in their gaberdines and the boys continued to attend cheder. Only the German constables in blue capes were new, and Polish and Jewish militiamen carried rubber truncheons in the streets. But the shortage of goods increased, the stores became more depleted, the women peddling fruit and provisions in Yanash's bazaar and the markets had almost nothing left to sell, and hunger began to be felt everywhere. German marks now mingled with Russian money, and the editorial writer of the Yiddish paper *The Moment* left off praising the Allies and began to vilify them. He prophesied the German occupation of St. Petersburg.

People came to worship at our house for the High Holy Days, but most of the women were unable to pay for pews. When Asher the dairyman rose to recite, both men and women began to wail. The words "Some will perish by the sword and some from starvation, some by fire and some by flood" had become

177

grimly vivid. One felt that Providence was preparing something terrible. Our Rosh Hashanah meal was meager, even though one is supposed to eat well on a holy day and especially at the beginning of the New Year. Father had not been called in very often for lawsuits, weddings, or divorces, though he was often consulted on questions of dietary law, for which he received no payment.

Nevertheless, the Germans did bring us one bit of luck, in the form of my brother Joshua's freedom. He no longer had to hide from the Russians under an assumed name. He could visit us, but every time he did, there was a quarrel between him and my father.

My brother and his worldly books had sown the seeds of heresy in my mind. We Jews with our belief in a God whose existence cannot be proved had neither country nor land to work, nor had we devoted ourselves to the study of trades. Storekeepers with nothing to sell now roamed the streets.

At 10 Krochmalna Street we had shared a hut in the courtyard with poor neighbors during the Feast of Tabernacles, but at No. 12, with families better off than we, the contrast between our food and theirs was all too evident. I especially remember my mother serving me a soup in which there was nothing "under the broth," as the saying goes. Reb Isaiah the superintendent, noticing this, threw in a pretzel, much to my consternation. All the same, I was grateful that he had been so considerate.

The war demonstrated for me how unnecessary
rabbis were, my father among them. From all the

towns and villages, rabbis and other ecclesiastics converged on Warsaw, dejectedly walking the streets in their silk gaberdines, looking for a piece of bread. Thousands of matchmakers, brokers, and small businessmen had no way of earning a living. Starving men dozed over their Talmud volumes in study houses and houses of prayer. The winter was cold and there was no fuel for the ovens.

In the house of prayer, some Jews explained that when Esau is stuffing himself, Jacob can find a small bone somewhere; but when Esau goes to war and suffers, it's the end for Jacob. If only God would take pity on Israel and send help! But apparently heaven was not thinking of Jews at that time.

I would like to tell about Joseph Mattes, who devoted himself to religious matters while his wife sold geese. Even before the German occupation, the cost of a goose had risen to twenty-five rubles. Who on Krochmalna Street could afford such luxury? Joseph Mattes, his wife, daughters, and their husbands were left penniless. While other goose dealers had managed to put something aside, Joseph Mattes had given his whole fortune to charity and the Radzymin rabbi.

The extent of his poverty was not known to those in the study house, and besides, the war had intensified individual selfishness. Men with full pantries worshipped alongside those who had nothing, but seldom thought of helping them. There wasn't actually that much food to share. Fear of the future haunted everyone. No one thought any longer that the war would end soon.

I became personally acquainted with hunger, and I noticed that the skin hung loosely on Joseph Mattes's pale face. But his son-in-law, another Israel Joshua, was even paler and more emaciated. Tugging at a barely sprouting beard, he hovered over the holy books, sighing and stealing glances beyond them. This delicate young man suffered from shame as well. He yearned to serve the Almighty, but hunger tormented him. Sinking ever more deeply into the Hasidic books, he twisted his sidelocks incessantly. What could he do about it, I wondered, this son-in-law living on his father-in-law's bounty and starving? Timid and weak, prematurely round-shouldered, he could do nothing but study and pray, and look into the *Grace of Elimelech* or *The Holiness of Levi* . . .

One Friday evening, Joseph Mattes, who had given his fortune toward Hasid banquets and the support of the Radzymin rabbi, slammed his fist on the table, shouting, "Men, I don't have the bread to usher in the Sabbath!"

His words were an indication of the times. Bread had to be substituted for the Sabbath wine when making the benediction.

For a moment there was silence, and after that, tumult, confusion. Reb Joseph's sons retreated into corners, painfully ashamed of what their father had said. Israel Joshua became chalk-white. Despite the collection of bread, fish, and Sabbath loaves that was taken up that night, nothing really changed. Paupers remained paupers, and benefactors were few. I felt terribly afraid that the same thing might happen to my father.

Like most of the rabbis, the Radzymin rabbi had moved to Warsaw, where he owned property. He was reputedly wealthy, but this was dubious, since real estate had ceased to provide income. I do not know whether he helped the Hasidim or not. Nevertheless, we were so much in need that Father paid a visit to the Radzymin rabbi's wife, the so-called "young rebbetzin." Unable to lend Father anything, she begged him to accept her diamond ring and pawn it. Father protested, but the rebbetzin swore: "By my life and health, take it!" showing him, at the same time, a Talmudic passage that prohibits the wearing of jewelry while others starve.

When Father, in his shame, returned home carrying the ring in a box, Mother made a face, perhaps from jealousy. But when Father pawned the ring, we bought flour, bread, and groats. Meat was too expensive. We began to use cocoa butter, which could be eaten with both meat and milk dishes.

The most difficult thing to bear at that time was the cold, and we could not afford to heat the apartment. Our pipes froze and it was impossible to use the toilet. For weeks, frost patterns decorated our windows and icicles hung from the frames. When I was thirsty, I broke off an icicle and sucked it.

At night the cold was unendurable. No amount of covering was enough. The wind, rustling through our apartment, made me think of goblins. Huddled in bed, I had fantasies of treasures, black magic, incantations *181* that would help my parents, Joseph Mattes, and everyone else who suffered. I imagined myself Elijah, the Messiah, and whatnot . . . Like the biblical Joseph, I filled storehouses with food and threw them open in the seven years of famine. A word from me made whole armies tremble, as well as their generals and the emperors behind them. I gave the Radzymin rebbetzin a basketful of diamonds.

It was too cold to get out of bed. Mother, my brother Moshe, and I never got up until late in the day, but Father forced himself to dress. The water for his ablutions froze. He rubbed his hands on the windowpanes and placed a pan of ice on the stove. He had learned to use the gas jet. The meter still required a forty-groschen piece but tea was his one luxury, although it consisted of hot water with just a pinch of tea leaves. Sugar was unavailable and he detested saccharin. Wrapped in a padded gaberdine, he drank his tea and studied, writing with frozen fingers. In *The Face of Joshua* everything was as it had been, and *Roar of the Lion* asked the ancient questions: Is the reading of *Shema* based on Mosaic or rabbinic law? Is one obliged to repeat all of it, according to Mosaic law, or only the first verse? Or the first section? Only there did Father feel comforted.

Before the war I used to buy him several small packs of cigarettes a day, and he also used to smoke a pipe. But now that cigarettes cost so much, he would fill his pipe with a peasant type of tobacco called Majorka. Smoking, drinking weak tea, he studied endlessly. What else was there but the Torah?

My brother Israel Joshua was living at home again, sleeping on a table in my father's study, where the cold was worse than it was outside. My mother covered him with whatever she could find.

In spite of the terrible frosts, mice invaded our apartment, attacking books and clothes, leaping about at night with suicidal abandon. Mother obtained a cat, but this creature observed their activities indifferently, her yellow eyes implying, "Let them run. Who cares?"

Her mind seemed to be far away, she was always dozing, dreaming. "Who knows?" Father said. "She might be a reincarnation . . ."

Father took care of her respectfully. Wasn't it possible that she might have the soul of a saint? After all, a saint who sins is returned to earth for a while. The earth was full of transmigrant souls sent back to correct a single transgression. When Father ate, he would call the cat to him, and with an air of majesty she would allow herself to be coaxed, eating slowly and discriminatingly. Then she would look up gravely, as if to say, "If you knew who I am, you would feel honored to have me here . . ."

How could she go after mice?

The Journey

A problem

N 1917 our situation became so bad that
we could not stay in Warsaw any
more. We were hungry all the time.
There was an epidemic of typhus. My brother Israel
Joshua got a job at an educational organization, Haza-
mir, but his salary barely covered his own needs. Now
he became a "German"; he stopped wearing Orthodox dress and instead put on a derby and a short jacket.
My father, pious as he was, became furious with him.

As for my father, he got a job with the Radzymin
rabbi as editor of his religious writings. But the rabbi
did not like to pay much.

There was one hope for us, the town of Bilgoray,
where my mother's father was the rabbi. But Bilgoray
was under Austrian occupation and although Austria
and Germany were allies, the mail was irregular. Even
in normal times, letter-writing was not a favorite sport
of our relatives in Bilgoray. My mother dreamed that
Grandfather was dead.

It was known that there was more food in the
villages occupied by Austria than in German-occupied
territory, so tens of thousands of people waited in
front of the Austrian consulate in Warsaw, trying to

get visas. The line of waiting people was longer than the block itself and members of a family took turns holding their place. Our family waited for days, sometimes me, sometimes my mother, sometimes my brother Israel Joshua. At last, in July 1917, we received our visas! My mother, my brother Moshe, and I were to travel to Bilgoray; my father would join us later. As for Israel Joshua, he had different plans altogether. He was going with a girl in Warsaw and often stayed with her family for days at a time. He had begun to publish articles and stories in the Yiddish press of Warsaw. Bilgoray, a far-off village surrounded by forests, was not for him.

Now things were going well for us. I said goodbye to my friends and was ready to leave, but my shoes were in bad condition and I went to the cobbler in our courtyard to get them resoled.

The day was bright but the steps leading to his cellar room were dark, the corridor damp and moldy; I entered a tiny room littered with rags and shoes. The ceiling was crooked and the window small, the dirty panes patched with cardboard. I had thought that conditions were bad enough at home, but at least we had a spacious apartment with furniture and books. Here there were two beds covered with soiled bedding and on one of them, in the midst of its own filth, lay a newborn baby, wrinkled, bald, and toothless, like a miniature hag. The mother fussed at a stove that kept smoking, and a young, red-bearded man with sunken cheeks and a high forehead—yellowed like some of the leather about him—worked at the cobbler's bench.

Waiting while he resoled my shoes, I coughed from the dust and foul odors, and remembered something my brother had said about those who wore themselves out while idlers thrived. I was overcome with a sense of the injustice in the world, of young men going off to die or be wounded, of people whose constant work would not earn them a piece of bread, a shirt, or a baby crib. The cobbler, I knew, could not continue to struggle indefinitely. Sooner or later he would come down with typhus or consumption. And how could the baby flourish amid the smoke, dust, and stench?

It was my brother's opinion that there should be no rulers at all—that not only Nicholas, but Wilhelm, Karol, the English king, and all the rest, should be ousted and replaced by republics; wars should be abolished in favor of popular rule. Why had this never been done until now, and why were monarchs despotic?

When my shoes were repaired and I was out in the sunlight again, I felt guilty. Why should I be going on a wonderful trip while the cobbler was confined to his cellar? Today he still represents, to my mind, the ills of society. Although I was only a boy, I sympathized with the Russian revolutionaries. Nevertheless, I still pitied the Tsar, who was then being forced to chop wood.

My brother Joshua accompanied us in a droshky to the Danzig Station, which at that time was called the Vistula Station. He bought tickets for us, and we walked to the platform to await the train. It seemed strange to be leaving all the familiar places and

191

friends. But before long the huge locomotive, coughing and hissing steam, was ready for us, the awesome wheels dripping oil, a fire blazing within. Few people were traveling, and we found ourselves in an empty car. The German-Austrian border was only four hours away, at Ivangorod, or Deblin, as it was later called.

With a screeching of whistles, the train began to move. On the platform, my brother Joshua seemed to grow smaller.

It was thrilling to watch the world glide away, houses, trees, wagons, entire streets revolving and drifting backward as if the earth were a huge carousel. Buildings vibrated, chimneys rose out of the earth, wearing smoky bonnets. The towers of the Sobol, the famous Russian Orthodox church, loomed over everything, its crosses glittering like gold in the sun. Flocks of pigeons, alternately black and gold, soared above the spinning, whirling city. Like a king or a great wizard, I rode through the world, no longer fearing every soldier, policeman, Gentile boy, and bum.

As we went over a bridge I glimpsed tiny trolleys on another bridge, and people resembling locusts, the way the spies during Moses' time must have looked to the giants. Beneath us, on the Vistula, a ship sailed, and in the summer sky there were clouds resembling other ships, beasts, and piles of down. The train whistled again and again. Mother took cookies and a bottle of milk from a satchel.

"Say the benediction . . ."

Eating the cookies and drinking the milk, I forgot

war, hunger, and illness. I was in a paradise on wheels. If only it would last forever!

Even my friend Boruch-Dovid would not know about the existence of the parts of Warsaw and its environs that I now saw. I was amazed to see a trolley. If trolleys went this far, I could have come here myself. But it was too late now. We passed a cemetery that seemed like a tombstone metropolis. I'd faint with fear, I thought, if I had to walk there at night . . . or even during the day. But why fear the dead when you are on a moving train?

In Warsaw everyone was hungry, but the world we traveled through was beautiful and green. Mother kept pointing out the wheat, barley, buckwheat, potatoes, an apple orchard, a pear orchard—still unripe. She had been raised in a small town. Farmers mowed hay; women and girls squatting among the furrows dug out weeds, whose roots, Mother said, spoiled the grain.

Suddenly I saw a phantom-like, faceless creature, with arms outstretched. "What's that?" I asked.

"A scarecrow to frighten the birds."

My brother Moshe wanted to know if he was alive.

"No, silly." I saw that he wasn't alive, nevertheless he seemed to be laughing. In the midst of the field he stood like an idol, while birds circled him and screeched.

At dusk, a conductor appeared, punched our tickets, exchanged a few words with Mother, and observed with fascination what to him was our strange, un-

Gentile appearance. He was still bewildered, it seemed, despite the generations before him that had lived alongside the Jews.

In the fading light, everything became more beautiful, blossoms seemed more distinct, everything was green, juice-filled, radiant with the light of the setting sun, and aromatic. I recollected the Pentateuch verse: "The odor of my son is like that of a field the Lord has blessed."

It seemed to me that these fields, pastures, and marshes must resemble the land of Israel. The sons of Jacob were herding sheep nearby. Before Joseph's stacks of grain, other stacks bowed down. The Ishmaelites would arrive soon, riding camels, their asses and mules loaded with almonds, cloves, figs, and dates. The Plains of Mamre were visible behind the trees. God was asking Abraham: "Wherefore did Sarah laugh? Is anything too hard for the Lord? I will return unto thee and Sarah shall have a son . . ."

Suddenly I saw something and asked Mother what it was.

"A windmill."

Before we could get a good look, it vanished, as if by magic. But then it appeared again behind us, its blades spinning to grind flour . . .

We saw a river, but Mother said it was not the Vistula. Then there were cows, red, black, spotted, grazing. We saw sheep. The world seemed like an open Pentateuch. The moon and the eleven stars came out,

bowing before Joseph, the future ruler of Egypt.

Evening came and the lights were on at the Ivangorod Station when we arrived. We were at the border, beside a kind of highway, and Mother said, "We're in Austria." The station was full of soldiers who were not as tall, erect, or stiff-backed as the Germans. Many were bearded and seemed Jewish; they wore shoes and puttees. The tumult reminded me of the second night of a holiday at the Radzymin study house, when—to give their wives time to cook the holiday dinner—the men talked, smoked, and gesticulated. I felt at home. "Let's play chess," I suggested to my brother. We did not know how long we would have to remain there.

As soon as we had unpacked the chess set and sat down at a table to play, we were surrounded by soldiers and noncommissioned officers. Jewish soldiers asked us, "Where are you from?"

"Warsaw."

"And where are you going?"

"To Bilgoray. Grandfather is the Bilgoray rabbi."

A bearded soldier said he had been to Bilgoray and knew the Bilgoray rabbi.

One soldier stood beside me and showed me where to move, while another soldier helped Moshe. Finally it was the soldiers who played and we moved the pieces. Mother watched us with anxious pride. The soldiers were Galician Jews who probably wore fur hats and mohair coats on the Sabbath. Their Yiddish had a somewhat flatter sound than what was spoken in Warsaw. One soldier let my brother hold his sword and try on his cap.

I do not remember how we spent that night, but the following day we rode to Rejowiec in another half-empty railroad car.

In Rejowiec, where there was a Russian prisoner-of-war camp, I saw unarmed Russians with unkempt hair and shabby uniforms digging under Austrian guard. Austrians and Russians crowded the depot commissary, which was kept by a Jew with a trimmed beard.

Twisting their tongues to speak German, the Russians sounded as if they were speaking broken Yiddish. Certain Jewish soldiers among them did speak Yiddish.

The Russian prisoners had built a new track from Rejowiec to Zwierzyniec, and continued working at it the next day, as we rode. While Nicholas chopped wood, Cossacks were learning Yiddish. For all anyone knew, the Messiah *was* on his way.

Bilgoray

The Rabbi of Bilgoray,
Isaac Bashevis Singer's grandfather

E rode past evidence of the Russian retreat—charred forests in which an occasional half-burned tree still sprouted green leaves and twigs. Despite three days' travel by train, I continued to watch everything with love and curiosity: fields, forests, gardens, orchards, and villages . . . One tree with uplifted branches seemed to be begging for a gift from heaven; another, bowing low, appeared to have abandoned all hope of good from anything but the earth itself. Still another, completely black, was a disaster victim, everything gone but its roots. Whether it hoped for anything or was merely involved in dying, I could not know. My thoughts sped on with the wheels, stimulated by every tree, shrub, and cloud. I saw hares and squirrels. The odor of pine needles mingled with other scents, both exotic and recognizable, although I did not know from where. I wished that like some hero in a storybook I might leap from the moving train and lose myself amid green things.

Recently a short track had been laid between the villages of Zwierzyniec and Bilgoray, and although it was not finished, it was in use. Our train was a small, *201* toylike locomotive with tiny wheels, and in the low flatcars there were benches where Bilgoray passengers sat.

Everyone in the car looked sunburned, their clothes had a sun-faded appearance. Many of the men had red beards and were dressed in gaberdines, and I felt related to them all.

"Bathsheba . . ." someone called. "The rabbi's Bathsheba . . ."

Although I knew this was my mother's name, I had never heard her called anything but "Listen here"—which was my father's method of gaining her attention, since the Hasidim did not approve of addressing a woman by name. Bathsheba, for all I knew, was merely a biblical name that no one actually used.

Here they were calling her Bathsheba and the women were embracing and kissing her. Although a dream had convinced her of her father's death, no one had confirmed it; yet now she asked them, "When did it happen?"

After a silence they began to tell her not only about her father but about her mother and sister-in-law, Uncle Joseph's wife, Sarah. Grandfather had died in Lublin, Grandmother a few months later in Bilgoray. Sarah and a daughter, Ittele, had died of cholera, and two cousins, Ezekiel and Itta Deborah, the son of Uncle Itche and the daughter of Aunt Taube, had also died.

In this sun-drenched day, in the midst of pine woods, in this green paradise, the terrible news came to her, and Mother began to cry. I too tried to cry, feeling it appropriate, but the tears would not come. I cheated, wetting my eyes with saliva, though no one was looking at me, nor did they care whether I wept or not.

Suddenly everyone shouted; the rear cars had jumped the track. There was a long wait while the cars were set back on the track with poles. That Sabbath, everyone agreed, a prayer of thanks would have to be offered. Other passengers, less fortunate than we, had been known to perish on this makeshift railroad.

Between Zwierzyniec and Bilgoray, the scenery was beautiful. We rode through forests and meadows, and passed an occasional straw-roofed hut or a white-washed house with a shingle roof. The train kept halting, to permit one person a drink of water, to allow another an interlude in the bushes; or the engineer would deliver packages or chat with the various peasants who lived beside the tracks. The Jews treated the engineer as casually as if he were the Gentile who entered Jewish households on the Sabbath to light the ovens, and they asked him to make various stops for them. Once, during one of the prolonged halts, a barefoot Jewess in a kerchief came out of a shack with a gift of dewy blackberries for my mother. Having heard that the rabbi's Bathsheba was coming, she had brought the berries as a present. Mother had no appetite, but my brother Moshe and I ate them all, staining our lips, tongues, and hands. The years of starvation had left their mark on us.

Though Mother had praised Bilgoray, it was even prettier than her descriptions. From a distance the pinewoods surrounding it looked like a blue sash. The houses were interspersed with gardens and orchards, and before them stood massive chestnut trees such as I had never seen anywhere in Warsaw, including the Saxony Gardens. There was a sense of serenity in this town that I had not encountered before, a smell of fresh milk and warm dough. Wars and poverty seemed far away.

Grandfather's house, an old wooden loghouse painted white, with a mossy roof and a bench beneath the windows, was near the synagogue, the ritual bath, and the poorhouse. The family came out to welcome us, the first to run up being Uncle Joseph, who had inherited Grandfather's position. Uncle Joseph always ran, even though he was thin and bent. He had a milky beard, a beaked nose, and bright, birdlike eyes, and was dressed in rabbinical gaberdine, wide-brimmed hat, and low shoes with white stockings. Without kissing Mother, he cried out, "Bathsheba!"

A stout woman, Aunt Yentel, his third wife, waddled after him. His second wife, Aunt Sarah, had died a year and a half before, and his first had died when he was sixteen. Aunt Yentel was as stout and relaxed as Uncle Joseph was narrow and agile. She seemed more the rebbetzin than he the rabbi. A horde of red-haired children trailed behind them. I who had fiery red hair myself had never seen so many redheads at once. Until then my red hair had made me a novelty in cheder, the study house, and the courtyard; it had seemed exotic, like

my mother's name, my father's occupation, and my

brother's talent for writing. But here there was a whole flock of redheads, and the reddest among them was my uncle's daughter Brocha.

I was taken into Uncle's large kitchen, where everything seemed novel. The oven was as big as a bakery's, and Aunt Yentel was baking bread. Over the stove there was a hooded chimney, and on the stove there was a tripod on which a pot boiled. Flies crawled over a huge lump of sugar on the table. The scents of leavening and caraway filled the air. My aunt offered us some prune cake, which tasted like it was made in Paradise. My cousins Avromele and Samson took me into the courtyard, which was actually a garden with trees, tall nettles, weeds, and wild flowers of all colors. There was also a sleeping porch; I sat down on the straw-mattress bed, and it seemed to me I had never known such luxury. The sounds of birds, crickets, and other insects rang in my ears, chickens wandered about in the grass, and when I raised my head I could see the Bilgoray synagogue and beyond it fields that stretched to the forest's edge. The fields were all shapes and colors, squares and rectangles, dark green and yellow . . . I wished I could stay here forever.

The New Winds

A water carrier in a Jewish town

PHEAVAL marked Bilgoray, for so long successfully obscured from the world by my grandfather. Now its immutability was being threatened from many sources. A few months after we arrived, a Zionist society was established by the young people of the town. Certain young men indicated Bolshevik sympathies. Youthful worshippers at the house of prayer separated into two factions: the Mizrachi and the Traditionalists. My friend Notte Shverdsharf formed a pioneer division, the Hachalutz or Hashomer, and was trailed by hordes of children who called themselves Zebim, wolves. Whether larger cities showed the same tendencies as Bilgoray, I did not know. In the streets, boys passing each other would straighten up, click their heels in the Austrian manner, and shout, "*Chazak!*—Be strong!"

All kinds of evening discussions and parties were now being held in this town, which a year before had been a sleepy Jewish community. A Warsaw dramatic company performed *Shulamit* in the firehouse. The Austrians, who had started a school in Bilgoray, erected a theater in the marketplace. The Hasidim resented my uncles because they made no objection to this, did not drive out the heretics as their father would have done. But his sons lacked his personality and strength.

Jonah Ackerman, a third-rate lawyer, opened a library of worldly books in his house. He was the son of an enlightened man, a sharp-tongued opponent of Hasidism. When the Gorlitz rabbi had come to town to be greeted with music and bells, old man Ackerman, standing in his doorway, had hissed, "Idol worshippers!"

Jonah Ackerman was dedicated to nothing but compromise. A lawyer, he said, must not antagonize his clients. In three-quarter-length surtout, Hasidic hat, and with a pointed yellow beard, he spent his Sabbath in the same Gorlitz study house that his father had vilified. Raised on Russian literature—not on Tolstoy and Dostoevsky, but on those before them, like Lomonosov and the writers of moralistic works—he had a principle to apply to everything, and enjoyed moral discussions. A pedant with a calligraphic handwriting, he was especially attentive to grammar and syntax.

His personality seemed to have evolved from print. He had an amazing memory, was said to know certain codices by heart, and owned numerous dictionaries and lexicons. Finally he decided to open a library and ordered both Yiddish and Hebrew volumes. He was in general a pure-hearted old bachelor, old-fashioned and a bit eccentric.

By this time my knowledge of Yiddish writers included Mendele Mocher-Sforim, Sholem Aleichem,

Peretz, Asch, and Bergelson, but I had not read them thoroughly. Now I read enthusiastically the poetry of Bialik, Chernichovsky, Jacob Cohen, and Schneyur, and had an insatiable desire for more. I had never forgotten the two volumes of *Crime and Punishment* that intrigued me so, even though I scarcely had understood what I was reading.

Now, under the apple tree in the garden, I would start a book one day and finish it the next. Often, sitting on an overturned bookcase in the attic, I would read among old pots, broken barrels, and stacks of pages torn from sacred books. Omnivorously, I read stories, novels, plays, essays, works written in Yiddish, and translations. As I read, I decided which was good, which mediocre, and where truth and falsity lay. At that time America was sending us sacks of white flour and Yiddish translations of European writers, and these books fascinated me. I read Reisen, Strindberg, Don Kaplanovitch, Turgenev, Tolstoy, Maupassant, and Chekhov. One day I devoured *The Problem of Good and Evil* by Hillel Zeitlin. In this book Zeitlin gives the history and summation of world philosophy and the philosophy of the Jews. Sometime later I discovered Stupnicki's book on Spinoza.

I remembered how Father used to say that Spinoza's name should be blotted out, and I knew Spinoza contended that God was the world and the world was God. My father, I recalled, said that Spinoza had contributed nothing. There was an interpretation by the famous Baal Shem that also identified the world with the Godhead. True, the Baal Shem had lived after

Spinoza, but my father argued that Spinoza had drawn from ancient sources, which no Spinoza disciple would deny.

The Spinoza book created a turmoil in my brain. His concept that God is a substance with infinite attributes, that divinity itself must be true to its laws, that there is no free will, no absolute morality and purpose—intrigued and bewildered me. As I read this book, I felt intoxicated, inspired as I never had before. It seemed to me that the truths I had been seeking since childhood had at last become apparent. Everything was God—Warsaw, Bilgoray, the spider in the attic, the water in the well, the clouds in the sky, and the book on my knees. Everything was divine, everything was thought and extension. A stone had its stony thoughts. The material being of a star and a star's thoughts were two aspects of the same thing. Besides physical and mental attributes, there were innumerable other characteristics through which divinity could be determined. God was eternal, transcending time. Time, or duration, controlled only the modi, the bubbles in the divine cauldron, that were forever forming and bursting. I too was a modus, which explained my indecision, my restlessness, my passionate nature, my doubts and fears. But the modi too were created from God's body, God's thought, and could be explained only through Him . . .

As I write these lines today, I am critical of them, being familiar with all the defects and lapses of Spinozism. But at that time I was under a spell which lasted many years.

I was exalted; everything seemed good. There was no difference between heaven and earth, the most distant star and my red hair. My tangled thoughts were divine. The fly alighting on my page had to be there, just as an ocean wave or a planet had to be where it was at a specific time. The most foolish fantasy in my mind had been thought for me by God . . . Heaven and earth became the same thing. The laws of nature were divine; the true sciences of God were mathematics, physics, and chemistry. My desire to learn intensified.

Other boys, Notte Shverdsharf and Meir Hadas, were not, to my astonishment, at all interested in my discoveries. My absorption amazed them, just as their indifference shocked me.

One day Notte approached me and asked if I would be willing to teach Hebrew.

"To whom?"

"Beginners. Boys and girls."

"But what about Mottel Shur?" I asked. "He is the Hebrew teacher."

"They don't want him."

I still don't know why they didn't want Mottel Shur, unless it was because he had quarreled with the founders of the night school that now sought to employ me. Mottel had a weakness for telling people what he thought of them; also, he boasted too much— and perhaps he asked too high a fee. I hardly dared accept the position, knowing it would embarrass my mother and cause consternation in the town. But something made me accept.

In the private home where the first class was held, I discovered that my pupils were not, as I had assumed, children, but young men and women, and somewhat more of the latter. The girls, my age and even older, came dressed in their best clothes. I faced them in a long gaberdine, a velvet hat, and with dangling sidelocks. How, since I am naturally shy, I had the nerve to accept this assignment I do not know, but it has been my experience that shy persons are sometimes unusually bold. I told them everything I knew about Hebrew. The class created a furor in Bilgoray—to think that the rabbi's grandson had lectured worldly boys and girls on the Hebrew language!

After the lesson, the girls surrounded me, asking questions, smiling. Suddenly I was dazzled by a particular narrow face, a dark girl with coal-black eyes and an indescribable smile. I became confused, and when she asked me a question I did not know what she was saying. Many novels and a lot of poetry had filled my mind by then; I was prepared for the turmoil that writers call "love" . . .

Shosha

Isaac Bashevis Singer, age twenty-two;
at about this time, he began to write

IN the days when we used to live at 10 Krochmalna Street, I mostly stayed home at night. Our courtyard was dark and the small kerosene lamps in the hallway gave more smoke than light. The stories my parents told about devils, demons, and werewolves made me afraid to go out, so I would remain indoors and read.

In those days, we had a neighbor called Basha, who had three daughters: Shosha, who was nine; Ippa, five; and Teibele, two. Basha owned a store that stayed open until late in the evening.

In the summertime the nights are short, but in winter they are very long. The only place I could go at night was Shosha's apartment, but to get there I had to pass through a dark corridor. It took only a minute, yet that minute was filled with terror. Luckily, Shosha would almost always hear me coming, running and breathing heavily, and would quickly open the door. At the sight of her, I lost all fear. Shosha, though she was a year older than I, was more childish. She was fair, with blond braids and blue eyes. We were drawn to each other because we loved to tell each other stories, and we also loved to play together.

The moment I entered the apartment, Shosha took out "the things." Her toys consisted of articles discarded by grown-ups: buttons from old coats, a teakettle handle, a wooden spool with no thread left, tinfoil from a package of tea, and other such objects. With my colored pencils, I often drew people and animals for Shosha. Shosha and her sister Ippa admired my artwork.

There was a tile stove in Shosha's apartment behind which there lived a cricket. It chirped the nights through all winter long. I imagined that the cricket was telling a story that would never end. But who can understand the language of crickets? Shosha believed that a house imp also made its home behind the stove. A house imp never does anyone any harm. Sometimes it even helps the household. Just the same, one is afraid of it.

Shosha's house imp liked to play little tricks. When Shosha took off her shoes and stockings before she went to sleep and placed them near her bed, she'd find them on the table in the morning. The house imp had put them there. Several times when Shosha went to bed with her hair unbraided, the house imp braided it while she was asleep. Once when Shosha was playing at casting goat shadows on the wall with her fingers, the shadow goat jumped off the wall and butted her on the forehead. This, too, was a trick of the house imp. Another time Shosha's mother sent her to the baker to buy fresh rolls and gave her a silver gulden to pay for them. Shosha lost the gulden in the gutter and came home frightened and crying. Suddenly she felt a coin in her hand. The house imp tweaked her left braid and whispered into her ear: "Shlemiel."

I had heard these stories many times, but they never failed to make me shiver with excitement. I myself liked to invent things. I told the girls that my father had a treasure that was hidden in a cave in the forest. I boasted that my grandfather was the King of Bilgoray. I assured Shosha that I knew a magic word that could destroy the world if spoken. "Please, Itchele, please don't say it," she would beg me.

The trip home was even more frightening than getting to Shosha's. My fear grew with the stories we told each other. It seemed to me that the dark hall was full of evil spirits. I had once read a story about a boy who had been forced by the demons to marry one of their she-devils. I was afraid that it might happen to me. According to the story, the couple lived somewhere in the desert near Mount Seir. Their children were half human and half demon. As I ran through the dark corridor, I kept repeating words that would guard me against the creatures of the night:

"Thou shalt not permit a witch to live—
A witch to live thou shalt not permit."

When we moved to 12 Krochmalna Street, there was no question of visiting Shosha at night. Also, it was not fitting for a Hasidic boy, a student of the Talmud, to play with girls. I missed Shosha. I hoped we'd meet on the street sometime, but months and years passed and we did not see each other.

In time Shosha became for me an image of the past.

I often thought about her during the day and dreamed about her at night. In my dreams Shosha was as beautiful as a princess. Several times I dreamed that she had married the house imp and lived with him in a dark cellar. He brought her food but never let her go out. I saw her sitting on a chair, to which she had been tied with rope, while the house imp fed her jam with a tiny spoon. He had the head of a dog and the wings of a bat.

After the First World War, I left my family in Bilgoray and returned to Warsaw. I began to write and my stories appeared in newspapers and magazines. I also wrote a novel called *Satan in Goray* in which I described the devils and demons of olden times. I was married and had a son. I applied for a passport and a visa to emigrate to the United States, and one day they arrived. I was about to leave Warsaw forever.

A few days before I left, my feet led me to Krochmalna Street. I hadn't been there for years and I wanted once again to see the street where I grew up.

Few changes had taken place, though the buildings were older and even shabbier. I peered into some courtyards: huge trash cans; barefoot, half-naked children. The boys played tag, hide-and-seek, cops-and-robbers, just as we had twenty-five years ago. The girls occupied themselves with hopscotch. Suddenly it occurred to me that I might be able to find Shosha. I made my way to the building where we used to live.

God in heaven, everything was the same—the peeling

walls, the refuse. I reached the corridor that led to Shosha's apartment, and it was just as dark as in the old days. I lit a match and found the door. As I did so, I realized how foolish I was being. Shosha would be over thirty now. It was most unlikely that the family would still be living in the same place. And even if her parents were still alive and living there, Shosha would surely have married and moved away. But some power I cannot explain forced me to knock on the door.

There was no reply. I drew the latch (as I had sometimes done in the old days) and the door opened. I entered a kitchen that looked exactly like Basha's kitchen of twenty-five years before. I recognized the mortar and pestle, the table, the chairs. Was I dreaming? Could it be true?

Then I noticed a girl of about eight or nine. My God, it was Shosha! The same fair face, the same blond hair braided with red ribbons, the same longish neck. The girl stared at me in surprise, but she didn't seem alarmed.

"Who are you looking for?" she asked, and it was Shosha's voice.

"What is your name?" I said.

"Me? Basha."

"And your mother's name?"

"Shosha," the girl replied.

"Where is your mother?"

"In the store."

"I once lived here," I explained. "I used to play with your mother when she was a little girl."

Basha looked at me with large eyes and inquired, "Are you Itchele?"

"How do you know about Itchele?" I said. A lump stuck in my throat. I could barely speak.

"My mother told me about him."

"Yes, I am Itchele."

"My mother told me everything. Your father had a cave in the forest full of gold and diamonds. You knew a word that could set the whole world on fire. Do you still know it?"

"No, not any more."

"What happened to the gold in the cave?"

"Somebody stole it," I said.

"And is your grandfather still a king?"

"No, Basha, he is not a king any more."

For a while we were both silent. Then I asked, "Did your mother tell you about the house imp?"

"Yes, we used to have a house imp, but he's gone."

"What happened to him?"

"I don't know."

"And the cricket?"

"The cricket is still here, but it chirps mostly at night."

I went down to the candy store—the one where Shosha and I used to buy candy—and bought cookies, chocolate, and halvah. Then I went back upstairs and gave them to Basha.

"Would you like to hear a story?" I asked her.

"Yes, very much."

I told Basha a story about a beautiful blond girl whom a demon had carried away to the desert, to

Mount Seir, and had forced to marry him, and about the children that were born of the marriage, who were half human, half demon.

Basha's eyes grew pensive. "And she stayed there?"

"No, Basha, a saintly man called Rabbi Leib learned about her misfortune. He traveled to the desert and rescued her."

"How?"

"An angel helped him."

"And what happened to her children?"

"The children became completely human and went with their mother. The angel carried them to safety on his wings."

"And the demon?"

"He remained in the desert."

"And he never married again?"

"Yes, Basha, he did. He married a she-demon, one of his own kind."

We were both silent again, and suddenly I heard the familiar chirping of a cricket. Could it be the cricket of my childhood? Certainly not. Perhaps her great-great-great-granddaughter. But she was telling the same story, as ancient as time, as puzzling as the world, and as long as the dark winter nights of Warsaw.